Some people talk about faith. Some write and read about faith. And some people model faith. Jon and Ken model it. This book is a treasured glimpse into the faithful lives of two faith-filled people. They are my heroes. I recommend this book with no hesitation.

MAX LUCADO, pastor and bestselling author

Selfishness may well be the deadliest disease we bring into marriage. While Ken and Joni are quick to admit their imperfections, I can't think of a more selfless couple to learn from. I pray that many will read this book and benefit from their example as much as I have.

FRANCIS CHAN, author and speaker

From the time I first read *Joni* back in the 1970s I've marveled at the amazing journey of faith that Joni has traveled. Hers has not been a story of gliding down an easy path, but down a tough and seemingly impossible road. Her resilience has given hope to millions. The story of Joni and Ken falling in love and their marriage is a beautiful love story, but it's a story that is anything but saccharine-like sentimentality. It's the kind of sacrificial and unconditional love that only God can supply. They are cherished friends and beautiful examples of the kind of faith that weathers storms and endures the harshest realities. When you read their story, you'll have a new perspective about yours.

MIKE HUCKABEE

I first met Joni a few years after the accident that dramatically altered her life. But until I read this book, I had little appreciation for the challenges she and Ken have faced together: the normal stresses of marriage complicated by quadriplegia, a life lived in the spotlight, and her recent life-threatening illness. My goodness — and the rest of us think we have problems! Their hard-won fidelity stands as an inspiring and redemptive example. Thank you, Joni and Ken, for baring your lives in this most vulnerable way.

PHILIP YANCEY

Joni & Ken will grip couples and singles as they contemplate what commitment really means. What I love about this story is that it includes the greatest story ever told — that Jesus set the example of endurance in the face of deep trials. Joni and Ken are remarkable witnesses to the strength that comes when we surrender to the One who cares for our every need.

FRANKLIN GRAHAM, president & CEO of Samaritan's Purse and the Billy Graham Evangelistic Association

Ken and Joni are a couple who model real love and real commitment, in a real marriage between two *very* real people. Their "love story" will motivate you to excel still more in your marriage, *and* it is one of those books you are going to give to your friends. Buy a case of their books and encourage your family and friends. This is a *great* story that needs to be made into a movie!

Dr. Dennis Rainey, CEO of FamilyLife

The words "for better, for worse, for richer, for poorer, in sickness and in health" don't begin to capture the challenges that Ken and Joni have encountered in their marriage. But they have overcome those challenges through steadfast commitment to one another and continual surrender to Jesus Christ. Theirs is a love story for the ages.

Jim Daly, president of Focus on the Family

Joni and Ken have allowed us an up-close-and-personal glimpse into their marriage — a thirty-year journey characterized by challenges few of us can imagine. As we witness the pruning, purifying, transforming effects of trials in their lives, we dare to believe our own sufferings and flawed human relationships can press us closer to Christ, mold us into His likeness, make us more fruitful, and fit us for eternity.

Nancy Leigh DeMoss, author and radio host
of *Revive Our Hearts*

All those years ago, we had the privilege of sharing some music at Joni and Ken's wedding. We even had a trio with the bride, Joni — singing Pelle's song, "Unfailing Love." And what an unfailing love their journey has been! Unfailing love for the Lord and His work, and unfailing love for each other. We thank God for their amazing example and testimony, and we say, "Thanks, Joni and Ken! We see Jesus in your love and in your lives!"

Evie and Pelle Karlsson, Christian musicians

Joni and Ken are loved throughout the globe for their groundbreaking ministry to the paralyzed and broken, yet their lives together have not been without immense challenges. Here is an honest story of commitment, surrender, and selfless love that will inspire and give hope to all who long to know if their day-to-day struggles and victories matter to God. These two lives beautifully lived will speak right to your heart from theirs.

Ravi Zacharias, author and speaker

This profoundly beautiful love story shreds the deceptive "happily ever after" myth and portrays something far more powerful, fierce, and eternal. Joni and Ken's story will leave an indelible mark on you, heart and soul. It has on me, and I am deeply grateful to my friends, Joni and Ken, warriors both.

SHEILA WALSH, Women of Faith speaker and author
of *God Loves Broken People*

In this book, a remarkable couple tells a remarkable story that radiates their devotion to Christ and therefore to each other. It makes you laugh, cry, and praise God as it so well reflects the highs and lows of Christian marriage.

R.C. SPROUL

We've always known that Ken and Joni face the unique challenges of quadriplegia, fame, and ministry demands. Now, through the pages of this book, we get to peek inside their marriage to see its struggles and triumphs. Best of all, this book shows that what has made their marriage work can also make *our* marriages work — tenderness, patience, unselfishness, and, most importantly, the power of the Holy Spirit to generate these things in us when our resources have run out.

NANCY GUTHRIE, Bible teacher and author of *Holding On to Hope*

For every couple who faces adversities and challenges, *Joni & Ken* is a must-read story of hope and encouragement that reflects God's heart for marriage.

STEPHEN ARTERBURN, founder and chairman of New Life
Ministries and bestselling author

Poignant and profound! Joni and Ken's love story will transform your understanding of "for better, for worse" and "in sickness and in health." Through almost unimaginable adversity, their tender commitment to Christ and each other is elevating. This book is sure to change many lives.

JUNE HUNT, founder, CEO, and CSO (Chief Servant Officer)
of Hope for the Heart

The integrity of making a vow has lost much of its impact in our world today. When you read this book by Joni and Ken, you will have a picture of what God intended when He instituted the covenant relationship of marriage.

VONETTE BRIGHT, cofounder of Campus Crusade
for Christ International

Jesus never said, "I am the power cord; you are the iPhone." He said, "I am the vine; you are the branches." Only Joni can so gently remind us of the kind of faulty thinking that positions God as our charger instead of as the very source and sustenance of our lives. This self-sufficiency heresy in my heart has been dealt a lethal blow by Joni and Ken's courageous telling of their story. Thank you, friends.

NICOLE JOHNSON, author and dramatist

Joni & Ken is an engaging, eye-opening, and heart-touching love story that cried out to be told. Nanci and I love Joni and Ken. While I love all of Joni's books, this one is unique, containing much that is new to me. *Joni & Ken* is honest, penetrating, at times riveting, and ultimately transcendent.

RANDY ALCORN, author of *Heaven* and *We Shall See God*

I'm so thankful to Ken (and Joni) for his openness, honesty, and transparency in letting us see beyond the brave and godly persona of Joni to what God has brought about through their marriage, Joni's cancer, and the unending day-by-day difficulties — simply because of a paralysis that leaves one entirely dependent on others. Jack and I were there at the beginning of this romance — a romance that serves as an example of our Savior's love for His bride, the church. You two are *our* heroes of the faith.

KAY ARTHUR, cofounder of Precept Ministries International

Joni and Ken's words seem wet with tears ... I think they're mine. Their journey is tender, honest, and soul-searching, and it quickly winds itself around your heart. It's a stunning love story laced with hurts, hardships, and a great deal of hope. Come and see what the Lord hath wrought.

PATSY CLAIRMONT, author of *Stained Glass Hearts*

I love this book. Ken and Joni open up their life — the good and the bad — in a way that is gripping, challenging, and hope-giving. Reading their story made me want to trust Jesus more. It made me want to love my wife more sacrificially. It reminded me that God can use the worst trials in life for our good. Whether you are single, engaged, or married, I highly recommend this book.

JOSHUA HARRIS, pastor and author

JONI&KEN

AN UNTOLD LOVE STORY

KEN & JONI EARECKSON TADA

with LARRY LIBBY

ZONDERVAN®

ZONDERVAN.com/
AUTHORTRACKER
follow your favorite authors

ZONDERVAN

Joni & Ken
Copyright © 2013 by Ken and Joni Eareckson Tada

This title is also available as a Zondervan ebook. Visit www.zondervan.com/ebooks.

This title is also available in a Zondervan audio edition. Visit www.zondervan.fm.

Requests for information should be addressed to:
Zondervan, *Grand Rapids, Michigan 49530*

ISBN 978-0-310-33673-0

International Trade Paper Edition

Any Internet addresses (websites, blogs, etc.) and telephone numbers in this book are offered as a resource. They are not intended in any way to be or imply an endorsement by Zondervan, nor does Zondervan vouch for the content of these sites and numbers for the life of this book.

Published in association with the literary agency of Wolgemuth & Associates, Inc.

Cover direction: Curt Diepenhorst
Cover photography: Dan Davis Photography
Interior design: Beth Shagene

Printed in the United States of America

13 14 15 16 17 18 19 /DCI/ 21 20 19 18 17 16 15 14 13 12 11 10 9 8 7 6 5 4

If any couple draws inspiration from this book,
may it be credited to the staff and volunteers
of Joni and Friends who run our Family Retreats.
These amazing men and women have a heart
to mend marriages, safeguard families affected by disability,
and show the weakest couple
that Jesus Christ really is the Answer.

❧

CONTENTS

A DIFFERENT KIND
OF LOVE STORY

The world has probably been singing love songs since Jubal, sixth from Adam, began experimenting with his newly invented musical instruments, tootling on his hand-carved flute or plucking his prototype harp while his long-suffering and more practical brother Jabal was out in the fields looking after the family livestock.

Have you missed the story of Jubal and Jabal? It's right there, what there is of it, at the beginning of your Bible in Genesis 4:19 – 21.

There weren't all that many women in the world in those days, but it's an even bet that Jubal attracted some positive feminine attention with this intriguing new activity. What had he called it? *Music?* Sitting by a murmuring stream under a spreading willow, running swift fingers across plant-fiber harp strings, he probably sang tuneful ballads about the big empty world newly wounded by the fall and not far removed from the memory of paradise, needing love, sweet love.

There have always been love songs, and the lion's share of them through the long ages have been wistful, sad, and melancholy. Someone falls in love with someone else, glorying in a brief, improbable burst of happiness, only to have something go wrong. A misunderstanding. A rejection. A betrayal. A slow dwindling of the flame that blazed so brightly. And then the music comes, the song from the bruised heart, telling the old, sad story of what had so briefly flowered, what almost was, what never was, what might have been, and what was lost forever.

The songs have a million titles, and after the fiasco at the Tower of Babel, the world found itself with songs in a bewildering multiplicity of languages and dialects.

In years to come, disappointed lovers would be singing in Etruscan, Indo-European, Sanskrit, and Proto-Germanic about cheating hearts, last dances, moonlit walks, heartbreak hotels, try-to-remember Septembers, and silhouettes on the shade.

It's the same today. If you have any knowledge of songs from thirty, fifty, or even seventy-five years ago, just hearing a fragment of melody can weave a web of nostalgia or call up a particular shade of melancholy from some forgotten archive of memory.

> *The shadow of your smile, when you have gone ...*
>
> *Are you lonesome tonight, do you miss me tonight? ...*
>
> *Eleanor Rigby, picks up the rice in the church where*
> *a wedding has been ...*
>
> *I really am indeed, alone again (naturally) ...*
>
> *I remember the night, and the Tennessee waltz ...*
>
> *One is the loneliest number that you'll ever do ...*
>
> *My heart will go on ...*
>
> *I fall to pieces ...*
>
> *I need your love. Godspeed your love to me ...*

Back in the 1940s, a popular song tapped into a theme that has been repeated over and over through the centuries:

> *Missed the Saturday dance*
> *Heard they crowded the floor*
> *Couldn't bear it without you*
> *Don't get around much anymore.*[1]

A February 2009 article in the *Los Angeles Times* was titled, "For the lonely: 150 songs for sobbing on Valentine's Day." In the introduction, the author promised "150 of the saddest songs in the world, subjectively selected and specially arranged for maximum depressive potential."[2]

Why are so many love songs and love stories sad?

They're sad because we pin our fondest hopes and dreams on a romantic relationship, but life hardly ever falls together the way we had hoped or imagined. We might "wish upon a star," along with Jiminy Cricket, but wishes are generally wispy, tenuous things that don't hold up to the rough-and-tumble of real life.

Love songs reawaken that soul-deep desire within us for a shining, transcendent experience of romantic love. Through that experience, we hope to escape the disappointments of a broken and mostly cynical world. But then the dream ends, the hope slips away — and we have to return to a shades-of-gray world that seems ordinary, lonely, and just a little bleak.

Why did more than 750 million people around the world sit in front of their TVs thirty years ago to watch the wedding of Britain's Prince Charles and Lady Diana Spencer? Was it just the fairy-tale spectacle of it all, with the carriages, the glittering uniforms, and the ivory silk wedding gown with its twenty-five-foot train?

Yes, it was certainly a spectacle.

But it was more than that, wasn't it?

I think many people wanted to set aside their cynicism and really believe — if only for a moment — in a man and woman living happily ever after together in a palace somewhere. Why? Because maybe if *that* marriage worked, perhaps some of the magic, some of the romance, some of the happiness, might spill over into so many other love stories — stories that began so well, showed such promise, raised such hopes, and faded so quickly.

That's what makes the love story in *this* book worth thinking about.

It isn't some sweet, shallow love song, but it has music with deeper roots and a more celestial melody than most of us could imagine. There are no artificial ingredients in this account, with a union movie orchestra playing strings in the background. It is authentic life, complete with disappointments, pain, disillusionment, struggle, tenacious faith ... and what you might call a surprise ending.

Yes, it begins in the traditional way, with a handsome young man and a lovely young woman falling in love with each other. There is a courtship, a wedding, a honeymoon, world travels, and the promise of a bright future.

Other than that, the story is anything but normal. Joni, who has become known all over the world for her writing, speaking, singing, and painting accomplished with a brush held in her teeth, was paralyzed from the neck down in a diving accident in 1967 when she was just seventeen years old. At age thirty-two, she had pretty much given up the idea that any man would or could look beyond her wheelchair and her disability to see her as a prospective lover and wife.

But she hadn't reckoned on Ken Tada.

A high school history teacher and football coach, Ken saw in Joni a beautiful woman with an even more beautiful personality and spirit. Most important of all, he saw a woman with a great passion for the One they both called Lord and Savior — Jesus Christ.

This was the girl of his dreams.

But life is more than a dream, and Ken, with proverbial stars in his eyes, had no concept of the difficult path that lay ahead of them. Joni had a much clearer picture of it all. Women usually do.

So they married.

And the account on the following pages dips into their story here and there, skipping back and forth through the years, showing some of the scenes from their life together.

It's a marriage that began strong, ran into hard times, faded a little, hit much harder times, and ... well, I don't want to give away the ending. We need stories like Ken and Joni's. We need to hear about dreams that don't end, even when trouble comes in the night to scramble the story.

This book is essentially about two people who had every reason on earth not to fall in love and marry each other in the first place ... whose marriage faced obstacles beyond what most of us could imagine and innumerable justifications for giving up ... who stayed together when their impossible obstacles unexpectedly became impossibly more difficult ... and who found a way, through it all, to attain to a new level of love rather than simply surviving or grimly hanging on.

Remember the song Susan Boyle sang to win *Britain's Got Talent* and launch her stellar YouTube fame? *I had a dream my life would be so different from this hell I'm living...*

We all dream dreams and know very well that they don't always work out. Life is particularly hard on high expectations. Things hardly ever fall together the way we would have scripted them. The fact is, if we put our hope in a certain set of circumstances working out in a certain way at certain times, we're bound to be disappointed because nothing in this life is certain.

So what's the solution? To give up on dreams?

No, it is to realize that if we belong to God, there are even bigger dreams for our lives than our own. But in order to walk in those bigger dreams, we may face greater obstacles than we ever imagined and find ourselves compelled to rely on a much more powerful and magnificent God than we ever knew before.

That's what happened with Ken and Joni Tada.

Some people might call it a fairy tale, but it's really a miracle.

And a miracle is better than a fairy tale.

LARRY LIBBY
Richland, Washington

CHAPTER ONE

THE GIFT

God, who foresaw your tribulation,
has specially armed you to go through it,
not without pain but without stain.

C. S. LEWIS

DECEMBER 6, 2011

Out of the corner of his eye, Giuseppe Bellisario saw the gleaming white Toyota van roll up into the handicap spot in front of his modest storefront restaurant tucked in the far right corner of the Agoura Hills Town Center. And smiled.

The bold-white, edged-in-scarlet letters over the entrance shone out in the California twilight: GRISSINI RISTORANTE.

Grissini.

Italian for "breadsticks."

But not just any generic, garden-variety breadsticks. His restaurants had always been known for their signature long, thin, artistically shaped grissini. And for warm greetings and assiduous service. He had always seen to that.

Impeccably dressed as always, he straightened his jacket and collar and glanced into the dining area, feeling a small surge of pride. No, little Grissini's didn't compare to his legendary establishments of years gone by, at least not in fame, size, location, or celebrity clientele. Back in the 1970s, his first place, Giuseppe's, had been the talk of the town, gracing the corner of Beverly and

Sweetzer, just off Wilshire between Hollywood and Beverly Hills. Those were the days! Giuseppe's had been the "it" place to go. Frank Sinatra would show up for lunch sometimes. Laurence Olivier would slip in for an early dinner.

Other celebrated restaurants followed, but none had been as exciting as Giuseppe's, with actors, writers, and directors popping in for those fabled Hollywood power lunches. He had a special table for them, tucked back in the kitchen where they could have privacy, dine quietly, sip a glass of Chianti, and savor all the simmering fragrances.

Then the years slipped away — so quickly! — and the time came when he told himself he was getting too old and ought to sell. And just like that, he cashed it all in and found himself retired. A nondescript Chinese restaurant now stood where Giuseppe's had once sent out its Italian fragrances and romantic aura into the night. Bellisario had stepped back from the whole business, intending to travel with his wife, Barbara, intending to "do other things." Funny thing about all those intentions. Somehow none of those "other things" seemed half as fun or satisfying as what he had done throughout his long career. So, perhaps surprising no one (and certainly not Barbara), he opened yet another restaurant, this time in a sleepy, out-of-the-way shopping center. In Agoura Hills of all places.

No, there weren't many celebrities dropping by these days, but the cuisine was as heavenly as ever, and besides that ... just look who was about to wheel through his doorway.

A sturdy Japanese man in his early sixties, clad in a brown jacket and a tan "Wild Adventures" baseball cap, emerged from the driver's side, stepped around to the back passenger-side door, pushed a button, and watched as the door slid open and a ramp descended.

Giuseppe waited for a moment as the man backed the power wheelchair down the ramp onto the pavement. Then, with consummate timing, Giuseppe stepped through the door into an abnormally chilly Southern California evening. Greeting the man with a handshake, and then a hug, he bent down to kiss the cheek of the pretty blonde woman in the power chair. Then, with a flourish that seemed second nature, he swung the glass door of his restaurant wide open to his friends.

"*Buonasera.*"

A gust of warm air, scented with oregano, fresh bread, and Christmas candles, enveloped them.

"Merry Christmas, Giuseppe," the woman said.

"And Merry Christmas to you, *caro.* Your table is waiting. Always."

Inside, Giuseppe's little "retirement project restaurant" was a vision of white tablecloths, linen napkins, spotless silverware, glittering Christmas lights, and candles glowing in red glass containers. The voice of Dean Martin crooning in the speakers wrapped around them like an old favorite bathrobe.

> *Volare, oh oh,*
> *E cantare, oh oh oh oh,*
> *No wonder my happy heart sings.*
> *Your love has given me wings* ...[3]

With no hesitation, the woman in the wheelchair, wrapped in winter coat and scarf, powered up to a table along the wall. Her table. A small brass marker on the wall read "JONI EARECKSON TADA."

Ken Tada, taking his seat, was already thinking of the menu.

"Giuseppe, do you have the veal tonight — on the bone — the one with the mushroom sauce?"

"Vitello marsala?"

"I think so."

Joni just smiled, drinking it all in.

> *We can sing in the glow of a star that I know of,*
> *Where lovers enjoy peace of mind.*
> *Let us leave the confusion and all disillusion behind* ...

Dear old Dean Martin. She truly *did* feel that glow tonight. In some strange, inexplicable providence of God, she felt happier than she had for years.

Cancer, she told herself, not without a note of wonder, *was a gift*.

CHAPTER TWO

"WITH GREAT PURPOSE"

This is God's universal purpose for all Christian suffering:
more contentment in God and less satisfaction in the world.
JOHN PIPER

JUNE 20, 2010

Cancer hadn't felt like a gift in the beginning.

No, not at all.

Joni had been noticing the odd deformity in her right breast for over a month, a slight indentation, as though the skin were tacked to something inside. Strange. Maybe even troubling. But she had ignored it — or tried to. As the days went by, however, the indentation seemed deeper. On a Sunday afternoon in June 2010, she couldn't ignore it any longer, and she called Judy Butler, her longtime friend and assistant, into the bathroom to check out the irregularity.

"Do you feel a lump, Judy?"

Judy felt, looked away, felt again. "Yes." She looked into Joni's eyes. "Yes ... there's definitely something there." A pause. "Shall I call Ken?"

Joni nodded. "Please."

Stepping inside the bathroom, Ken took in the scene at a glance. Joni's and Judy's expressions in the vanity mirror told him more than he wanted to know. *What now?* At Joni's instruction, he too felt for an irregularity and found one. A definite lump. Something foreign. Something hard where nothing hard should be.

He looked up, making eye contact with both of them in the mirror.

Looking across at her misshapen breast in the glass, Joni said, "I really don't have time for this!" For just a moment, it struck everyone as funny, and they all laughed.

"I'll call Dr. Drew," Ken said. Scrolling through his contacts, he punched the cell number of Joni's personal physician, who immediately picked up. On a Sunday! And no, he didn't need to see them. They needed to get themselves over to Thousand Oaks Radiology first thing the next morning. He would call ahead and make arrangements.

So ... now they had an appointment. How quickly events seemed to move! On the short, thirteen-mile drive to the radiology center, Joni prayed, eyes open, watching the successive exits roll by. *Kanan Road. Reyes Adobe Road. Lindero Canyon Road. North Westlake Boulevard. The 23 Freeway.*

Uninitiated drivers in Southern California, flying along faster than they really want to go in the farthest right-hand lane, can suddenly look up in dismay to see the freeway dividing into two. And if the left four lanes are heading where you want to go, but you find yourself in the farthest right of four lanes bound in another direction, there's precious little opportunity to cross multiple lanes of racing, bumper-to-bumper traffic. In just a blink or two, you're swept along in another direction, toward another destination. Somewhere you couldn't have foreseen. Somewhere you never intended to go.

That's what this day was. This Monday like no other.

The freeway had divided, and Joni was being whisked away in a new direction. Fast. Toward ... what? Where? This much she knew. Her life would change that day. For better or worse, nothing would be the same after this.

A new thought intruded as Ken flipped the turn signal at Janss Road. So, life was about to change for her? *Maybe that wasn't so bad.* She suppressed the thought, only to have it circle back, stronger than before. *Could this be … her time, her release? Could this be THE exit she had longed for all those years? Did the exit sign read "HEAVEN"?*

✑

For a quadriplegic in a wheelchair, it was difficult, stressful — and in Joni's case, painful — to access the mammogram machine. When it was through, she marveled how the technician's face could assume a perfect blank. No expression at all. Like a mannequin.

"We'll need an ultrasound," was all she said.

In an adjoining room, a second technician moved the scanner across Joni's breast, clicking something in her instrument, taking measurements, but allowing Joni to view it all on the digital screen.

And what she saw, intruding into healthy breast tissue, was a large, dark mass.

Threatening. Like a storm cloud on the horizon.

Joni tried to keep her voice steady. "Is it a lesion?"

"Yes," the technician said, wrapping up the exam. "A doctor will be in right away to see you." Alone in the examining room, Ken and Joni exchanged glances, Ken pursing his lips and moving them back and forth the way he always did when he was agitated. (She knew him so well!) He held Joni's hand, knowing that she knew it but couldn't feel it. It was for his sake as well as hers.

Dr. Ruth Polan swept into the room, charts in hand, explaining that Joni had "a large, suspicious mass with irregular edges" and that she would have to have a biopsy. Joni took a deep breath and repeated the words back to her, making sure she had heard correctly.

The doctor pulled out a well-thumbed list of oncological surgeons; at the very top was Dr. David Chi.

"One of the best," she said, quickly adding, "but you'll have difficulty getting in to see him. His schedule is always full. I could recommend some alternatives ..."

Ken and Joni decided immediately to try for Dr. Chi. There must be a good reason why his schedule was always full. And why not? After all, this was God's itinerary, so why not check to see if He'd booked first class? They made the call from the imaging center, and it was as if the door flew wide open, amazing Dr. Polan but not Ken and Joni. Dr. Chi would see them in just a couple of days.

So just that quickly, they were linked up with a cancer surgeon.

A surgeon.

The freeway had split, and they were speeding toward a different destination than they had intended just twenty-four hours before. And there was no going back to the way it was.

Out in the van, Ken embraced Joni, wiped tears from his eyes, and blew his nose. Joni had no tears at all. The events of the past twenty-four hours seemed — distant, somehow.

Ken shook his head back and forth. "What next?" he said. They had been married twenty-eight years and traveled together on six continents, but this was uncharted territory, off the edges of any map they had ever seen. What did it say on the margins of those old world maps, where the known world fell away into mystery? *Here be dragons.*

No. Wrong thought, wrong image. Not dragons at all. God saw the whole map of their lives, right to the very edges and beyond. He could handle any dragons. Even one with a name like Cancer.

Joni suddenly remembered something Alan Redpath, a British pastor and author, had written.

"Remember what Redpath said, Ken? I think I can quote it. 'There is no circumstance, no trouble, no testing, that can ever touch me until, first of all, it has gone past God and past Christ, right through to me. If it has come *that* far, it has come with great purpose.'

"Ken, I believe this cancer has come with great purpose."

Ken nodded, wiping his eyes again. "Yeah," he said, "but didn't he also say something about the Christian life getting harder the further you go?"

JUNE 23, 2010

Joni sat at her office computer at the International Disability Center, staring at a blank screen. Was there anything as empty in all the world as an empty Word document? With the assistance of her speech recognition software, she had the ability to compose text as quickly as most able-bodied people can type.

Well and good. But what should she *say*?

Earlier that morning, she had wheeled into Doug Mazza's office, her calm, competent COO at Joni and Friends, to tell him the news. The first words out of her mouth (before she'd even had time to think about it) were, "Doug, God must be up to something big." Joni was in transition; that much was obvious. But transition to what ... and where? Would she be in heaven in a few months? *On her feet again ... running, running across meadows as wide as the sky ... taking long autumn walks with her daddy, feeling the leaves crunch beneath her feet ... dancing with the angels.* Maybe, and maybe not. Whatever God had in mind for her, the agenda had certainly changed, and that much was almost a relief. She had something new to focus on now, besides the brutal, take-no-prisoners, never-ending battle with chronic pain.

Her staff needed to know too. And she wanted them to know. Wanted their prayers most of all.

And she'd need them. Just yesterday, Dr. Chi had performed the needle biopsy. She'd heard the word *needle* and thought nothing of it. *How bad can a little needle be?* she thought. Forget that! It was a nail gun into her breast — twice to get a good sample! It was her first indication that this wasn't going to be easy.

Lord, give me words. Your words. Where should I start?

Almost immediately the answer came. *Start with gratitude.* Of course. That was where so many good things began. She spoke aloud, watching the words leap to life in twelve-point Times New Roman on the monitor.

"You have always been so faithful to pray for Ken and me — especially for my health. But today I bring before you a new concern.

"I have breast cancer ..."

It was strange, almost surreal to speak those last four words into existence in her document. It was almost as though setting them down in that cyberdocument gave reality and finality to something that had seemed more like a bad dream. The freeway she was on had a name, *Cancer*, but it didn't have a final destination. Not yet.

"Ken and I have been assured by our doctors that there are many new treatments for breast cancer, and we are very hopeful for a successful surgery and a full recovery."

Again she paused. Were they really hopeful? Yes ... yes they were. But not necessarily hopeful in the circumstances. It was hope in Jesus Himself. *The Resurrection and the Life.* She looked again at what she had written. Now it was time to say how she felt about all this. But what did she feel? Had she put it into words yet — even in her own mind? This was no time for banalities or happy-talk phrases. This was life and death; this was war. Besides, her staff knew her too well; she had always been honest with them, and they'd see right through any window dressing. *OK, then ... how do I really feel about this, Lord? Show me.* She began speaking again.

"You have often heard me say that our afflictions come from the hand of our all-wise and sovereign God. And although cancer is something new, I am content to receive from God whatever He deems fit for me, even if it is from His left hand. Better from His left hand than no hand at all, right?! Yes, it's alarming. But rest assured that Ken and I are utterly convinced that God is going to use this to stretch our faith, brighten our hope, and strengthen our witness to others."

Joni knew her memo would raise many more questions

among the staff than it answered. What stage was the cancer? Had it spread beyond her breast? Would her quadriplegic body, increasingly frail and wracked by over twelve years of chronic, searing pain, be able to endure yet another assault? And how in the world does a paralyzed person do chemo?

Who knew? God knew. And Joni knew Him. So did David, when he wrote: "Yes, my soul, find rest in God; my hope comes from him. Truly he is my rock and my salvation; he is my fortress, I will not be shaken" (Psalm 62:5 – 6).

On the following Monday, Joni went into surgery.

JUNE 29, 2010

Blog posting on the Joni and Friends website:

Joni is resting in the recovery room with Ken after a successful procedure. The initial doctors' reports indicate that it appears some lymph nodes were affected by the cancer and Joni will need chemotherapy to follow up this surgery. So let's give praise to our loving God for bringing Joni and Ken through this. And let's ask Him to give them yet more grace and peace for the next steps.

JUNE 30, 2010

Another blog post:

More than 36 hours have passed since Joni's surgery, and she continues to make great improvement. Today Joni is preparing to leave the hospital and plans to be at home in her own bed by this evening. She writes, "I've been so blessed by reading the many cards and e-mails and the blog posts on Joni's Corner. Ken and I are absorbing as much information as we can from the nurses and physical therapists here at the hospital before we leave. I'm just very much looking forward to sitting up in my wheelchair and looking at life from a 90-degree angle rather than in bed! I want to thank the many people who have been praying for me. Judging from the progress on my healing after surgery, plus my high spirits, God is doing great things through your prayers!"

Next steps for Joni and Ken involve meeting with a medical oncologist to determine the kind and course of chemotherapy she will undergo. Joni adds, "Please pray for the many decisions we will be making over the next few days as we begin battling this cancer."

JULY 3, 2010

Ken and Joni's longtime friends, Al and Margaret Sanders, their son Jim and their daughter Peg, had been in the hospital waiting room, praying for Joni during the course of her surgery.

The next day was Sunday, July 4, and Al had called on Saturday to ask if they could bring some food over to the house that day and visit for a while. Would Joni be up to it? Ken smiled at the prospect. "We'd love it," he said. "Come anytime. You guys are just like family."

"Better than family," Al replied with a chuckle. "We know when it's time to go home."

It just so happened that Saturday, the third, was Ken and Joni's twenty-eighth wedding anniversary. Later, they would remark to each other that it was the sweetest either of them could remember, though neither could say just why. Maybe it was the tender, careful way Ken emptied the drains from Joni's chest, still raw and bruised. Or the way he kept adjusting the pillows to keep her right arm elevated, the arm where so many lymph nodes had been removed. Maybe it was because they just sat together in the living room, having no other plans. Funny, how the conversation took them places they had never been before. It was good to just be quiet sometimes too, watching the afternoon sunlight play over the lattice, sparkle from the pool outside, and weave dreamy shadow patterns on the carpet. And the little hummingbirds had seemed especially busy, darting around their feeders but never quite getting their fill.

And the Sanders and Peg were coming tomorrow. Wasn't God

good! Who would have thought there would be a little Fourth of July party just days after the surgery? Around 8:00 p.m., Ken, who had been reading a history of the Battle of the Bulge, stirred himself. He should do some things to get the patio ready for guests. Good grief, here it was July, and he hadn't even gotten out the cushions for their patio chairs yet.

"I'm going out to the garage," he called to Joni in the bedroom. "I'll just be a minute or two."

Out in the garage, Ken realized his task might involve a little more excavation than he'd thought. Pushing the garage door opener, he climbed into the car and turned the ignition.

And immediately heard Joni's voice. Singing.

In the house? No, of course not. Over the car speakers. A CD? No, there was nothing in the player. This was *radio*. KKLA. Joni was doing one of her devotionals — one he hadn't heard before. But how could that be? He glanced at his watch. KKLA didn't broadcast her at that hour.

> *... In seasons of distress and grief*
> *My soul has often found relief,*
> *And oft escaped the tempter's snare*
> *By thy return, sweet hour of prayer!*[4]

This is amazing. I should go in and tell Joni, he thought. *I should turn on the radio in the house and let her listen.* But it was only a five-minute devotional. If he went into the house, he would miss her words. Somehow, he felt he was supposed to hear them. So he sat in the car, in the dim light of a single overhead bulb, listening to his wife through the car speakers.

"Life is hard for people in wheelchairs," she was saying. "But it's just as hard when you're the caregiver. So let me take a minute and pray. I want to pray, not only for you who are listening today who might have a physical disability, but let me pray for the people who help, OK?"

God spoke to him in that moment. "This is for you, Ken. Joni is praying for you."

What are the odds of this happening? he asked himself. *What are the odds of my being in the car at all at eight o'clock at night, and then turning the ignition and hearing my wife's voice, in stereo? Talking about praying for caregivers!*

"Dear Father in heaven," she prayed, "as I think of the cross Your Son endured for me, I thank You that the cross You have called *us* to bear will never, never be heavier than You have designed. Our cross is exactly the right size and weight for each of us, Your willing children. And daily as we pick up this cross and follow You, bless You for more than matching the burden with grace upon grace upon grace ..."

Grace upon grace. Ken knew beyond a doubt he was in one of those holy moments, when God seemed to be speaking directly to him, as if he'd been the only one in all of greater Los Angeles to hear this broadcast.

She went on. "And if at times our hardships seem too heavy a thing to daily endure, if these struggles are too much for our caregivers, too much for our husbands or wives or children to bear, then remind us that You are there right beside us, shouldering the worst of the weight of the cross. *Never* let us forget that You are with us through it all, whether it is we who are always sitting down in a stand-up world, or whether it is our caregivers who are always tending to our needs. And ... please, Lord Jesus, expand our vision, that we can appreciate the influence our trust in You is having on people, others who watch and learn, even from a distance. For that brings You glory! And brings rich and wonderful meaning to our days. In Jesus' name. Amen."

Ken switched off the ignition and sat for a moment. Then he closed the garage door and walked back into the house, a look of wonder on his face, the patio cushions forgotten.

"You'll never believe what just happened," he told Joni. After he had related the event, she looked into his eyes as if she'd somehow known about it all along and wasn't surprised at all.

"God's favor is resting on you, Ken."

He believed that, even though it didn't make much earthly

sense right then. God's favor was all around them, right in the middle of all the heartache, weakness, and fear. What had Joni said? *"Ken, I believe this cancer has come with great purpose."*

If she could believe that, then so could he.

JULY 4, 2010

It was one of those days when a person could reflect on the multiple millions of people crowded into Southern California and say, "I get it."

The sky was bright blue, with a few thin, wispy clouds; the day was warm and mild. A light breeze wafting through the valley blew just hard enough to make the roses along the cast-iron fence nod in affirmation.

Margaret Sanders had brought her keyboard, and after lunch she and Al set it up out on the patio. Joni sat in her chair in the shade of an umbrella, her arm propped up on a chair, allowing postsurgical fluids to drain from tiny ports under her arm. A phenomenal pianist, Margaret began playing hymn after hymn, and no one needed a hymnbook as they all sang along.

How wonderful, Joni mused. This was one of the most precious, extraordinary moments of fellowship she could remember for years and years. Sitting on the patio of her beautiful home with people who loved Jesus and loved them, looking out across the valley at the Santa Susana Mountains, singing hymns and praising God on a sunny Fourth of July. And it would have never happened, those people together in that place singing those words of praise, declaring God's worth with that particular tender joy, apart from her having breast cancer. Already, *already* God was working things — even hurtful, wounding things — together for good.

Ken was reflecting on how often he had sat in that same backyard on a summer evening listening to more abrasive music drifting across the valley — metal or rap blasting from one of his neighbor's stereos.

But not today. On this sweet summer Sunday, Mötley Crüe and Jay-Z had Martin Luther to contend with.

> *A mighty fortress is our God,*
> *A bulwark never failing;*
> *Our helper He amid the flood*
> *Of mortal ills prevailing ...* [5]

Our Helper! Yes. Joni prayed, *Praise You, Helper, Counselor, and Healer!* She couldn't remember having had a keyboard out on their patio before. It sounded extraordinarily good. Couldn't have been better in a cathedral. And those words, penned in Germany back in 1529, somehow seemed to have been written just for them, for that very day, with her arm propped up on a chair, draining fluids from a radical mastectomy. Surely God had that very moment in mind when he prompted Luther to dip a new quill into his inkwell and scratch out those lyrics on a fresh sheet of parchment.

> *And though this world with devils filled,*
> *Should threaten to undo us,*
> *We will not fear, for God hath willed*
> *His truth to triumph through us.*
> *The prince of darkness grim,*
> *We tremble not for him —*
> *His rage we can endure,*
> *For lo, his doom is sure:*
> *One little word shall fell him.*

Jesus. One little word? Two syllables? Perhaps. But a big enough word to make angels and devils alike bow in submission.

JULY 13, 2010

Through it all, Joni hadn't cried very much. In fact, she couldn't remember shedding a single tear since her diagnosis. It became one of those strange seasons when she felt like an outside observer of events in her life, some interested-but-coolly-objective third person, looking on her circumstances from a safe and hygienic distance. She'd heard people talk about that sort of thing before, how the mind sometimes grapples with traumatic events by casting a cloak of unreality over them. *This isn't me they're talking about. This isn't my mastectomy. This isn't my cancer. This isn't my crisis.*

That was part of it. But another part of it was her sheer determination to "see it through." She had seen crisis after crisis in her life. Was she going to let this new development overwhelm her? No! She would not. *This will NOT catch me off guard*, she told herself. *This will NOT throw me for a loop. This will NOT make a basket case out of me. God is in this. Of course He is. He is sovereign. I've always believed that. He is in control. I must trust Him at all costs.*

Those thoughts had come with just a little bit of pride. She commended herself on "doing it right" and "handling it all well" and "practicing what she had preached" for so many years.

But now she, Ken, Judy, and Kathy, Joni's sister, were crowded into the medical oncologist's absurdly small consulting room. And as Dr. Shahryar Ashouri took his seat and turned to face them, something about all those strong self-assurances and affirmations threatened to turn into Jell-O.

He spoke in quiet, matter-of-fact terms, sketching out the course of therapy she could expect in the coming days. He didn't speak in a medical monotone, nor did he seem unkind or unfeeling. It was the presentation of a professional who had gone over the same ground many times before, with countless other groups of shell-shocked, wide-eyed patients and family members. His detailing of the upcoming treatments was calm, factual, comprehensive, a bit dry ... *and utterly relentless.*

They would check her back into the hospital. Insert a surgical port into her chest. Begin a regimen of the chemotherapy drugs Taxotere and Cytoxan. She would be sick much of the time. She would lose her hair. She would lose her eyebrows. Her fragile bones would grow even thinner. She would be prone to lung and bladder infections. *Dear God, where did it stop?* She would be anemic and exhausted. She would have a dry mouth, mouth sores, and changes — possibly permanent — in her ability to taste and smell. She might experience severe diarrhea. She could expect rashes or hives or cracked nails or …

It seemed to go on and on. A veritable catalog of pain and suffering and loss and multiplied indignities, all spoken in that calm, clinical voice. And then he excused himself for a moment to check on another patient, left the room, and closed the door behind him.

For Joni, the closing door opened up a floodgate. Suddenly, it crashed in on her. All of it. The cancer. The surgery. The cancer-and-surgery-on-top-of-endless-pain-on-top-of-paralysis. The exhaustion. The loss of her breast. Going back to the hospital. A port in her chest — for *poison*. Losing her hair. Death, somewhere back there in the shadows. She collapsed into convulsive sobbing, weeping for all the losses and pain and disappointments here and now and long, long ago. The unshed tears of departed years.

"I can't do this … it's too much … I can't," she sniffed, her eyes and nose running.

Immediately, Judy walked over to Joni's chair, put her arms around her, and let her friend fall against her shoulder. Judy gave her a squeeze as sobs wracked Joni's frail body. She held her like that, murmuring words she might have whispered to a lonely, heartbroken child.

And then something unusual happened.

Ken stood up and said, "I'll do that."

Judy, more than a little surprised, looked up at him, uncertain at first about what he intended, and whether to let Joni go.

"Let me take over," he said quietly. And just like that, he did. Ken, her husband, *took over*. He put his strong arms around Joni, let her rest her head against his broad chest, and held her like that for a long time.

Joni, crying so hard she'd seemed oblivious to everything, wasn't oblivious to this. Something in her noted this … change.

This alteration in long-established realities. Through twenty-eight years of marriage, when it came to anything medical, Ken deferred to Judy. Judy was always there. Judy was a nurse. Judy had done it a thousand times. Judy knew the better way. Judy didn't mind.

Had he really just said, "Let me take over"? When had she heard him say that before? And somehow, this felt like something more than an impulse. She'd heard steel in his voice. This was something new. Possibly something wonderful. Perhaps even a gift.

And in that instant a new thought knifed through a fog of emotion and weariness.

I don't want to die.

CHAPTER THREE

THE PRAYER

*For I know the thoughts and plans that I have for you,
says the Lord, thoughts and plans for welfare and peace
and not for evil, to give you hope in your final outcome.*
JEREMIAH 29:11 AMP

BACK TO SUNDAY, APRIL 20, 1980

On most Sundays, being in church felt like a little breath of heaven.

But not every Sunday.

And this was one of those not-every-Sundays at Grace Community Church. Then again, maybe it was just *her*, feeling distracted, disjointed, and a little emotionally flat. Judy and Kerbe, one of Joni's many helpers through the years, had gotten her ready for church, and Judy, who knew her all too well, had asked her flat out, "Are you all right?"

One of the elders led the opening prayer. When he was done, Joni realized that even though she had closed her eyes and bowed her head, she really hadn't entered into the prayer at all and couldn't remember a word of it. The same elder led the hymn. She loved the hymn singing at Grace Community. Loved the harmony. The words. *Everything* about hymns of the faith. But this one? Sure, the words to "Blessed Assurance" stirred her soul, but the tune? It could, at times — depending on who was playing the piano — sound, well ... clunky. The downbeat could be so heavy, like marching to the beat of a drum.

This is my story, this is my song,
Praising my Savior all the day long;
This is my story, this is my song,
Praising my Savior all the day long.[6]

Joni gamely chipped in a strong harmony, but after stomping along on the second chorus, she gave up singing. It was too much effort. She would just listen. Judy, holding the hymnbook, gave her a quick sidewise glance.

Why did everything feel just a tad mechanical? Was it her imagination, or did it seem like the people around her weren't entering in today. *Or maybe it's you, Joni,* she said to herself. *YOU aren't entering in, and you're projecting your lack of enthusiasm on everyone around you.*

Still, something seemed missing today. A Sunday like flat Coke. No, that wasn't fair ... but something *was* different. During the announcements, there seemed to be more coughing, shifting, digging in purses, clearing of throats, murmuring, and rustling of papers than usual. Two women a few rows back were just talking right out loud, making no pretense of even a stage whisper. How inconsiderate.

Joni glanced over Judy's shoulder at the open bulletin. Oh no. Wouldn't you know it! They were going to have a guest speaker that day — someone she had never heard of. She had been looking forward to John MacArthur stepping up to the pulpit, opening his Bible, looking out across the congregation, gathering everyone in with an authoritative glance, and saying, "Let's look together in the Word of God at 1 Corinthians chapter 16 ..." Or wherever in the Bible he was, it didn't really matter.

He always began like that. Always cut right to the chase. There was no reflecting on yesterday's sports scores or news items, no banal observations on the weather, no cute stories or jokes or warm and fuzzy personal anecdotes to ease people into the message. It was — *boom* — "Open your Bibles to Hebrews 11 ..." And then he was off to the races, confident and sure of his material.

This was straight-up, no-apology, down-the-line expository preaching, and you could always count on a meaty, challenging message right out of the chute. Like that series on Romans. Oh, my goodness, how many weeks were they in Romans? Before it was over, it had seemed like Dr. MacArthur and the apostle Paul were team teaching. And people couldn't seem to get enough of it. For years now, people from all over Southern California had been driving up to Sun Valley in north Los Angeles to soak it in.

If he had been there that day, Dr. MacArthur wouldn't have let Joni's thoughts ramble. She was quite sure of that. Her pastor would have pulled her mind back from its wanderings and settled her on a focused, productive path. He would have helped rivet her back on the Word and locked her thoughts on the right frequency. But Dr. MacArthur was away at a conference. This was a guest speaker, and he *didn't* begin by saying, "Open your Bibles to ..." No, he began with a story. Which was OK, but ... a little long. And really, how in the world was he going to tie it in, and what was he going to tie it to? Or ... was he going to tie it in at all? He had evidently moved on to something else, but it wasn't what you'd call a smooth transition. More like a speed bump at thirty miles an hour.

In spite of herself, her mind wandered.

That couple two rows in front of her. He had slipped his arm around her, and she snuggled against him a little. Nice. His hand was touching her, lightly, brushing his fingers across her shoulder. And she liked it. How good would that be? How long had it been since a man had done that with her?

I wish I had someone. I'm almost thirty-two, and there's no one.

The power of dormant feelings stirred and awakened. Old pipe dreams. Love songs with "rainy days and Mondays" kind of lyrics. Memories of teenage boyfriends back in Maryland, in that misty Time Before prior to the accident. Longings. Desires. Disappointments. Fading hopes.

Stop it, Eareckson! Stop it right now!

She slapped her thoughts back into line, and pushed herself straighter in the wheelchair. *Attention! Front and center! This is a WORSHIP service. "We take captive every thought to make it obedient to Christ."*[7] *Get your mind back on the message.*

She tried … a little. But where was the message? It had evidently meandered down the tracks without her, and it was just a little late to get on board. She had no idea what he was talking about or where he was going. And he kept looking down at his notes with a bewildered expression on his face, almost like he had never seen them before.

Her eyes settled at random on the back of a man's head five or six pews ahead of her, drawn perhaps by his thick, black hair. In that instant, as if somehow aware that eyes were on him, he tilted his head slightly, revealing a strong jaw and the smooth, tanned curve of his neck. Leaning to the left, now in profile, he reached for a Bible in the rack in the pew.

Maybe he's bored too. Maybe he's going to read Scripture instead of trying to track with the sermon. A good-looking man. And sitting by himself.

What would it be like to have a man friend? Someone to be with. Talk to. A little romance? Things every woman longs for. Was it even possible for her, the way she was, the way life had worked out?

No. No. No. Stop it, Joni! She was losing this battle. And it must not happen. She would not sit there and squander a worship service on selfish notions. She would not … But it was taking a mountain of effort to pull her eyes away from the back of the man's head. That glossy, black hair. The athletic shoulders. He reminded her a little of Mr. Lee, her eighth-grade teacher she'd had a crush on.

The speaker droned on. *OK,* she told herself, *if I can't change my focus, I can change my purpose.*

She began to pray. *Father, You desire mercy rather than judgment. Those are Your words. Now be merciful to me, a sinner. And bless You for not judging me according to these empty, discontented thoughts. Stupid, silly thoughts that distract me from worshiping You. Be merciful and help me with this battle, for Your honor and for the benefit of this man, whoever he is.*

That was more like it. She had gained a little ground.

Father, I want to talk to You about this man for a minute or two. This good-looking guy with the nice black hair. This man You have known before the foundations of the earth. I pray for him! If he knows You, get him deeper into Your Word. Help him to obey. If he's dating somebody, convict him if he's messing around. If he's married (but I don't see a wife!), hold him to his vows. Don't let him get away with cheating, even if it's only in his thoughts. Strengthen him against the Devil and the world with all its temptations. Make prayer a big part of his life, and give him extra joy when he makes a stand for You.

Yes! She had regained her focus. Maybe this had been in God's mind all along. Maybe He had specifically brought her to church that day to intercede for that man, that stranger, who had needed prayer.

And Lord, if there are problems where he works, make his life shine as a real witness to his coworkers. If there is a lingering argument with his mother or father, resolve it, would You? Make his testimony at home consistent with what he believes here in this church.

She fixed her gaze on the man's head, the black and shining hair. Judy had glanced at her, probably thinking she was really into the speaker's message! A wave of peace washed over her as she sensed victory within grasp. She smiled to the Holy Spirit. *We're winning.*

The speaker was winding up his message. Where had the time gone?

Save him, Lord, if he's not in Your family. And if he already is, strengthen him. Refine his faith. Keep him from lies. Clear up his bad habits. Assist him in prayer. Sustain his health. Guard his mind. Deepen his friendships. Lord, make him into the man You want him to be.

Her heart bubbled up with honest-to-goodness joy. And maybe something more. She felt a sense of assurance that God had led her into those prayers, heard her petitions, and would answer them in His own way and in His own time. But she also knew He had enabled her to win the day over wandering, undisciplined, definitely unhelpful thoughts. And she had exalted Him on this Lord's Day, even if it was in a most unorthodox manner.

"Amen!"

The speaker had concluded his prayer, and people stood up to make their exit (was that relief she was sensing in the auditorium?). As if to compensate for a less than rousing sermon, the organist pulled out all the stops on a booming postlude, almost but not quite drowning out the sounds of people gathering books, Bibles, purses, and sweaters. Somewhere up ahead of her, the nice-looking man (Asian ... Hawaiian, perhaps?) had picked up his Bible and turned to leave.

"I'm starved!" Judy said with a smile, stepping out of the pew over Joni's foot pedals. "Let's hurry home for lunch."

"Let's!" Joni responded. The Asian man had stepped into the aisle. He had an athletic build. And a nice, almost shy smile. He was chatting with several people. Just for a moment, Joni wondered, *Should I approach him? Introduce myself? Maybe mention how I had prayed for him?*

Bad idea. *Very* bad idea. Of course not. He would think she was crazy, or being too forward or maybe making advances or something else just as unpleasant. Besides, it wasn't about her. The victory had been in getting outside herself, praying for him.

She decided to keep the incident between herself and God.

And somewhere, if she had known, God was smiling.

MAY 18, 1980

The memory of that Sunday battle in April had faded, and another worship service at Grace was wrapping up. This time, Dr. MacArthur had been in the pulpit and in top form, and Joni hadn't had any trouble locking into the Bible teaching. After the service, out in the foyer, one of Joni's friends introduced her to a handsome Asian-maybe-Hawaiian man … who looked strangely familiar.

Suddenly brightening, Joni asked him to turn around.

"Turn around?" he said, puzzled and not sure he'd heard right.

"Just for a minute. I want to see the back of your head."

He complied, turning slowly, and then back again. And ah, there it was. That nice, thick black hair. Joni explained that she had prayed for him, for the back of his head, in a church service where she had lost the thread of the message. They both had a good laugh over that. Ken looked pleased and just a little surprised.

They chatted for a few more minutes and went their separate ways. As Joni powered her wheelchair toward the exit, she realized she had already forgotten his name. And that wouldn't do. She pulled a neat 180 in her chair and circled back.

"I'm sorry," she said, "but I seem to have already forgotten your name. Mine's Joni."

"Oh, I know who *you* are," he said with a smile, his eyes crinkling pleasantly at the corners. "I'm Ken Tada."

And just that quickly, with a wave, he was gone.

JULY 7, 1980

It was not the way she had wanted to spend the rest of her July — inside her bedroom on a hospital bed. What an appalling waste of a beautiful Southern California summer.

Joni had been afflicted by pressure sores, the bane of those who are physically immobilized and compelled to spend an inordinate amount of time in a wheelchair, or any chair. It had to be treated, of course, and the main treatment was to get the weight off of it. And that meant extended time in bed, lying on special cushions to relieve pressure.

It was a long haul. And for someone already dealing with limited mobility issues — dreaming of sunshine, flowers, and sweet California breezes — the idea of weeks in bed was a heartbreaker.

On one of those long days, just after lunch, Joni had been on the edge of dozing off when Judy stuck her head in the room and announced she had a visitor. And suddenly Ken Tada appeared, walking into the room, smiling that million-dollar smile. Joni had been half asleep when Judy had announced his arrival, and even now, with afternoon sunlight streaming into the room, it all seemed to have a dreamlike quality about it. He'd heard she was stuck in bed and wanted to come by and say hello. But he also had something else in mind. Stepping back into the hall, he reemerged with some kind of strange wooden construction he had evidently created. It was an easel. And one that fit perfectly over a hospital bed!

"Now you can paint again," he said. "If you want to."

After he left, Joni closed her eyes a moment and thought about the goodness of God. On a restless, out-of-sorts Sunday, she had prayed for a total stranger, doing her utmost to push her thoughts away from herself.

And then God had brought that very man back to her own door, armed with a thoughtful, practical act of kindness to help her endure the long days of healing. How like Him that was!

And now — happy thought! — she had a new friend.

OCTOBER 15, 1980

Somebody's up to something.

Why had Ken Tada been invited to her birthday party? Joni was almost certain she could detect the hands of Carol and Twila behind this, two friends from church who were hosting the party at their town house.

And wasn't it funny how she kept running into him at church? And hadn't she seen him in the audience in Burbank at that Young Life function where she had spoken? But this birthday party thing was just a little too suspicious. She hardly knew him.

There was no doubt that Ken Tada was an attractive man. Probably Hawaiian. An island guy. And he had been so sweet to think of building that over-the-bed easel, all on his own. He sat on the sofa now at the town house, gesturing with a can of cola as he spoke. She liked the way he looked right at people when he was talking to them, giving them his full attention. She liked how he smiled so much, not just with his mouth, but with his whole face.

When she thought no one was looking, she stole a glance at him, studying his features. That thick black hair, 1980s full and bushy and over the tops of his ears, framed high, wide cheekbones, dark brown almond eyes. Judging from his strong neck and arms, he was an athlete. Was he reserved? Yes ... maybe even a little shy, even at this party among friends.

For most of the evening, she sat in a corner between the entryway and a living room chair, chatting with this person and that person, trying not to be overly conspicuous in her power chair. Was Ken going to walk over and talk to her, or at least make significant eye contact? Maybe not. Which was a little disappointing. The evening dwindled, and the guests began to drift away. Some tidy soul was gathering up plastic punch glasses and crumpled napkins. Most stopped to say good-bye and wish her a happy birthday as they funneled toward the front door.

Ken did too, but lingered.

Leaning against the wall beside her chair, he began chatting with her. *This is a man who is comfortable in his own skin*, she thought to herself. *I like that.* In the course of the conversation, she learned that he lived in a condo next door, was a history buff, taught social studies and government at a nearby high school, and coached football. *I knew it*, she told herself. *I was right about the athlete thing.* She also learned he wasn't Hawaiian at all; he was Japanese.

Finally, she told him she had to go — that she had an early morning the next day. Ken left, apparently to get his coat, and Joni said good-bye to Carol in the kitchen, thanking her for the party. Twila — bless her! — had knelt down to empty Joni's bulging leg bag.

As the bag drained slowly into a bottle, wouldn't you know it — Ken returned, coat over his arm. "I was wondering ..." he began. "How about if we continue our conversation over dinner next Friday night?" If he had noticed the leg bag operation, he'd given no sign of it. Not so much as a glance.

"I suppose so," she said, then instantly amended her answer. "Sure. I'd like to go."

"Can I pick you up about six?"

"That would be fine."

On the long road home, driving alone in her specially-equipped van, it suddenly occurred to her that she had accepted a date from a good-looking man, just like it was something that happened all the time. It had been so casual, so natural. Except for the leg bag thing. But then again, *that was life* for her, and there was nothing she could do about that.

She had learned a long time before that day that there was no pretense with a disability like quadriplegia. If Ken had any interest in her, he would have to deal with that part of it too, even on a first date.

Maybe it would scare him away.

Or maybe it wouldn't.

FRIDAY, OCTOBER 24, 1980

"Roses? For me? Who are they from?"

Kerbe slipped the tiny card out of its envelope and read it to Joni. "Looking forward to Friday ... Ken Tada."

Joni rubbed her nose against the soft yellow petals, sniffing the delicate fragrance. "Hmmm," she said. "Nice gesture."

"Is that all you can say?"

"I don't know ... I mean, don't you think it's a bit much? I hardly know him."

Kerbe sniffed her disapproval, but sensing Joni's uneasiness, she made no further comment. She set the vase on Joni's bedroom dresser, fluffing the blooms and greenery, and walked out of the room. Ken was a pleasant guy, Joni thought, but did he have to make such a big deal about going out to dinner? She had hoped he would have been more ... well, *casual* about it.

Joni stared at the roses. Well, he'd gotten the color right. Bright, sunny yellow roses were supposedly symbolic of joy and friendship. Maybe it was time she allowed a little of that joy to penetrate her heart. And friendship too, for that matter.

He didn't look casual at all, however, when he showed up at six o'clock on the button Friday night, dressed in a tailored blue suit and bearing yet another bouquet of flowers. Joni was glad she had dressed up a little too, in her white wool jacket and silk blouse. She hoped he wouldn't pop a button on his dress shirt when he lifted her in and out of the car.

Judy and Kerbe gave him a crash course in the essentials, explaining how to lift Joni single-handedly and straighten her in her wheelchair, how to tuck her jacket in the back so it wouldn't wrinkle, and how to pull down the inseams of her slacks. Ken listened attentively, showing concern for details.

He wheeled her outside to his car with Joni reminding him, as graciously as she knew how, to be mindful of the steel ramp, cracks in the sidewalk, and turning too-sharp corners. Her housemates watched, arms folded and somewhat amused, as Ken removed his jacket, rolled up his sleeves, hiked up his pants, and squatted by her chair to lift her. Slinging her arm around his neck as he'd been instructed, he surprised her with a mighty karate "hi-yah," lifting her to his chest and then setting her gently in the front seat.

"Hey," Joni joked, "it's a date with Bruce Lee!"

Judy showed him how to fold Joni's wheelchair and load it in the trunk, while Kerbe leaned into the car to straighten her jacket. "Have fun," she said with a smile as she pushed the door closed.

"You really aren't heavy at all," Ken observed as he backed out of the driveway. "Light as a feather."

"Oh, really? Judging from that weight-lifting exercise back there, I would have never known. HI-YAH!"

Ken steered with one hand while sliding a cassette into the

tape deck with the other. "Well, I *have* been working out a little," he admitted. "Lifting weights and stuff."

"Getting ready for tonight?"

"Maybe."

"OK. So how much do you train with?"

"Oh, about 175 pounds."

"A hundred and what!?"

"I wanted to make sure I didn't drop you," he said with a smile.

"Just so you understand, I don't weigh 175 pounds!"

He grinned. "Don't worry. I can tell how much you really weigh."

She returned his smile. So he knew how much she weighed? Of course he did. He'd held her in his arms already. On their first dinner date.

So what? she said to herself. She didn't have the luxury of the modesty and standoffishness that most women had on a first date. But that was her life, and it was what it was. What mattered was that there were no pretenses. What mattered was that she was out by herself with a man who evidently loved Jesus and who cared enough about her to go to all that extra trouble without making her feel in the least bit uncomfortable or strange about it.

It was a beautiful twilight in the southland, and traffic on the freeway moved swiftly, as easily and unencumbered as her conversation with this unassuming and delightfully ordinary guy.

❧

Marina Del Rey?

Nice! And a restaurant table overlooking the bay. *Yes!*

Joni looked out over the masts of hundreds of sailboats moored at the docks. The skyline of masts against the evening sky made a beautiful picture. *I should paint something like this*, she thought.

"You look nice tonight," Ken said, after the waiter had brought their water glasses and menus.

"Thank you," she said, inspecting her cuffs. "I usually wear this outfit when I'm speaking."

"Like at the Young Life dessert?"

"That's right. You were there, weren't you?"

"Uh-huh. And I liked what you said that night. About how we can relate to people whose circumstances are different from ours. Like your wheelchair. People don't have to be afraid of it." He picked up his menu and reached over to open hers. "Or of you."

"What do you mean?" she asked.

"Well, your wheelchair is one thing ... people not knowing how to relate to you — or what to say. And the fact that you're well-known — famous, really — is another. Lots of people think you have it all together. That you never struggle or have off days." He paused a moment to study his menu, made a quick decision, and closed it again. "But I don't need to be afraid just because you're Joni Eareckson or because you're different."

It wasn't a rehearsed speech, but Joni could tell he'd thought this through. And after thinking it through, he had laid to rest whatever apprehensions he may have had. Or at least, for now he had. She couldn't help but admire his confidence.

Ken ordered steak, and she went for the shrimp. Without a moment of self-consciousness or hesitation, he leaned across the table to give her a forkful of his appetizer. She asked for a drink, and he stretched his arm across the table again, lifting the glass to her mouth.

Just as if he'd done it a hundred times before.

They chatted about Joni and Friends, Judy and Kerbe, his students, and their mutual friends at church. When their dinners arrived, and before she could ask the waiter, Ken had his knife and fork poised over her plate, ready to cut up her shrimp. "May I?" he asked.

She couldn't get over how comfortable, how happy, she felt with this man.

"I would guess you've been around disabled people before," Joni suggested, scooping up another bit of shrimp.

"Well, yes and no." Ken leaned back from the table and dabbed the napkin to the corners of his mouth. *A gentleman,* Joni thought. "Sometime back when I was surfing the channels on TV," he said, "I came across a program on Special Olympics. There were some great shots of mentally challenged kids barreling down the track. Some stumbling. Some skipping. Others going flat out. And there were people at the finish line, cheering each one of those kids on. Everyone, I mean everyone, hugging each other. And then the announcer said something like, 'In a world constantly seeking perfection, where is there room for those who aren't?' Then he said, 'What really matters isn't winning but finishing.' I liked that."

He was quiet for a moment, reflecting on the memory, stroking the folded napkin.

He reached for his water glass. "So, that's when I signed up at my school to get involved in Special Olympics. I've only worked with them, officiating or whatever, for a couple of years." He put the glass down. "But dating someone in a wheelchair?" He smiled, leaning back in his chair. "No ... I've never done *that* before."

"Well," Joni replied, "there's something else you're going to have to do that you've never done before."

"What's that?" he asked, reaching for his wallet to pay the bill.

"My leg bag needs emptying."

Would it throw him — just a little? Apparently not.

"OK," he said. "Just tell me what to do."

Ken negotiated her wheelchair through the tables toward the door. They paused in front of the alcove leading to the women's room on the left and the men's room on the right.

He glanced quickly from the left to the right and said, "Uh, I guess we have a problem here."

"Yes. Well, I hadn't thought about this one."

"Come on, Joni, no jokes." He was whispering now, as several people walked around them, going in and out of the restrooms. "What do I do?"

Joni was still smiling. "Is this the part where you're not afraid, even though I'm different?"

He waited patiently.

"OK, OK. There's a bottle in my bag on the back of the wheelchair. Let's head outside and find a tree and empty this thing."

"A tree?"

"Well, it *is* more inconspicuous than a fire hydrant, don't you think?"

So it all began with laughter. What could have been awkward or uncomfortable somehow wasn't. Ken learned he could pretty much be himself with an already-famous Christian icon and household name who also happened to be paralyzed from the neck down. And Joni realized that she could enjoy an evening out with a handsome, good-hearted man who could look beyond her celebrity status and her disabilities to talk to her as a woman and a friend.

Friend sounded really good.

And so did that unspoken, back-of-the-mind thought that hinted at something more.

CHAPTER FOUR

IT'S NOT ABOUT US

*God is not unjust; he will not forget your work
and the love you have shown him as you have
helped his people and continue to help them.
We want each of you to show this same diligence
to the very end, so that what you hope
for may be fully realized.*
HEBREWS 6:10 – 11

FEBRUARY 8, 1982

Questions, questions, questions.

Over the last fifteen months, there had been any number of uncertainties swirling around Ken and Joni's courtship. And now, just as many questions surrounding their engagement.

Would it work? Did a marriage make sense? Even Ken and Joni's parents had misgivings. *How* would it work? Everyone said that marriage was a substantial life adjustment to begin with. Wouldn't it be exponentially more difficult when you added in the reality of a profound disability? Would the responsibilities of caring for a quadriplegic spouse (*"Remember, Ken, this is for the rest of your life ..."*) eventually be too much for Ken, wearing him down? Would the pressures and never-ending day-to-day routines put too much strain on a new marriage? What about Ken's teaching career? What about sex? Was that the elephant in the room nobody was talking about? Would they be able to have children? How would Ken handle living every day with someone famous? Would Joni find adequate time to invest in her marriage with a myriad of other things going on in her ministry?

And what did God think about it all?

It really came back to that last question; Ken and Joni were devoted Christ followers, and His will trumped every other concern. He had known both of them before they were born. Ken Tada and Joni Eareckson had been on His mind when He spoke the galaxies into being, spun the nebulae, and strolled with Adam and Eve through Eden in the cool of the day.

Ten years after Ken and Joni's marriage, Pastor Rick Warren would write a bestselling Christian book that began with a stark four-word sentence.

"It's not about you."

He would go on to write, "The purpose of your life is far greater than your own personal fulfillment, your peace of mind, or even your happiness. It's far greater than your family, your career, or even your wildest dreams and ambitions. If you want to know why you were placed on this planet, you must begin with God. You were born *by* his purpose and *for* his purpose."[8]

In the spring of 1982, mere weeks away from Ken and Joni's marriage, God began to speak to them as a couple about something much, much larger than themselves. Joni had invited her fiancé on a ministry trip to multiple nations in Europe. And in the course of that journey, all the questions surrounding their marriage began to slip, like pieces of a puzzle, into a larger context. If God had brought them together for a reason, what purpose did He have in mind for them *as a team*? What might they accomplish as husband and wife that they could never accomplish on their own as singles? It wasn't about them. It was about how God might be pleased to use them, together, for His purposes. If God was giving them a greater sphere of influence as Ken and Joni Tada, they needed to rise to that calling.

Ken Tada had grown up as a Burbank, California, boy who liked to stay close to home. As a high school senior, he had turned down a football scholarship to the University of Hawaii because he couldn't imagine himself so far away from Southern California. For a man who hadn't traveled much out of the country, the trip with Joni seemed like an absolute whirlwind. Accompanied by Judy and Jay, Joni's sister, they swept through London, Paris, and Amsterdam.

Big Ben solemnly tolling the hours under an overcast sky? The lights of Paris at night from a hotel balcony? Canals and windmills in Holland? It had all seemed so exotic and romantic.

And then came Romania.

APRIL 2, 1982

"We just crossed the Iron Curtain."

Joni had been peering out the window of the aging Aeroflot jet en route to Bucharest, and she spoke her thought out loud. Her comment brought a quick, hostile glare from the flight attendant.

"Shhh," Judy whispered, "I don't think we're supposed to say *those* words."

Flying over Germany and Austria, they had marveled at the glorious green landscape, tidy villages, and neat hedgerows. Halfway through their flight, however, the world below them morphed into a different reality. Even from an altitude of 15,000 feet, they could tell that the towns were poor and unkempt, connected by dirt roads rather than asphalt highways.

In a sullen red sunset they landed in Bucharest and taxied to the gate. This was the Bucharest of 1982, still clamped in the steel vise of the brutal Communist dictator Nicolae Ceaușescu, seven years before his overthrow and execution. The ostensible purpose for the visit was to meet with government officials on behalf of Joni and Friends, but the true focus was to connect with and encourage brothers and sisters in Christ and look into the plight of that nation's disabled population.

As they prepared to exit the plane, Ken looked out in amazement at a ring of armored vehicles and grim-faced soldiers carrying AK-47s. "Unreal," he said, pulling out his camera.

"Sir!" the flight attendant suddenly barked. "You must put away your camera. No photos are allowed."

Startled, Ken quickly complied. Yes ... truly this was a different world. London, Paris, and Amsterdam seemed like a planet away. And America? Southern California? It might as well have been in a different galaxy.

Romania in 1982 was a ravaged and denuded police state, with fear and dread hanging over the towns and countryside like a freezing fog. In J. R. R. Tolkien's universe, this was the land of Mordor, under the all-penetrating eye of an evil, highly paranoid, possibly demonic government. The once grand old boulevard leading into the city was potholed. And where were the cars? Very few and far between. Ken marveled to see horse-drawn carts clopping through the city, their drivers slump shouldered and sad, and even the horses seemed dispirited. Old-fashioned streetlights lined the boulevard, hinting vaguely of a grander bygone era, but now, not a single one was lit in the gathering gloom. The only lights in the city, it seemed, were the stoplights at intersections, but even many of those were darkened. Once-stately baroque buildings along the route appeared to be crumbling in on themselves and encrusted with grime. In some ways, it seemed more like Calcutta, minus the teeming crowds, than a European capital. A literal cloud, thick and dismal, hung over the once-magnificent city, heavy with the smell of leaded fuel and coal dust. The few people on the streets appeared like ghostly shadows clad in gray.

It brought to mind novelist Ray Bradbury's description of a land he called the October country: "... that country where it is always turning late in the year. That country where the hills are fog and the rivers are mist; where noons go quickly, dusks and twilights linger, and midnights stay. That country composed in the main of cellars, sub-cellars, coal-bins, closets, attics, and pantries faced away from the sun. That country whose people ... passing at night on the empty walks sound like rain."[9]

They had been directed to stay at the Intercontinental Hotel

in rooms predetermined by the Securitate. The hotel itself, however, didn't live up to the promise of its conventional, Western-
sounding name. It turned out to be yet another drab, dirty
building, probably erected in the 1950s. They were given rooms
on the second floor near the end of the hallway. Prewarned by a
Romanian friend, they assumed the suite was bugged. Before saying anything of consequence, they had been instructed to open
up both water faucets in the bathroom so the noise of the filling
tub would prevent the listening devices from picking up their
words.

As Judy removed Joni's coat, Ken whispered, low and urgent,
"Look!" They watched as he tried to move the mirror on the wall
above the dresser. It didn't budge. He tried to peek behind it with
no success. Stepping aside out of its view, he silently mouthed,
"It's part of the wall."

They looked at one another stunned, remembering the strange
door to the room next to theirs, a door with no room number.
What a ghastly feeling to think of some gray-faced Communist
apparatchik sitting in a dim little room staring at them through
a two-way mirror. Or was it just a camera? Whatever it was, it
gave one an eerie feeling.

But this side trip into Communist Romania was never
intended as a pleasure cruise. They had ventured into the heart
of totalitarian darkness for the sake of God's sons and daughters
who lived out their lives in that oppressive place, and for the disabled men and women who had to be there too, though no one
had heard of them or from them for years.

As Judy and Jay got Joni ready for bed in the next room, Ken
looked out the grimy hotel window at the scene below. The darkened windows of the building across the deserted street gaped
back at him like empty eye sockets. *What am I doing here?* He felt
a wave of homesickness for his sunny, bustling Southern California, so brimming with life.

At that moment, however, a fragment of Scripture intruded
into his thoughts. Something from the latter chapters of Matthew's

gospel, speaking of a time beyond time when all nations would be gathered before the King for judgment: "Then the righteous will answer him, 'Lord, ... when did we see you sick or in prison and go to visit you?' The King will reply, 'Truly I tell you, whatever you did for one of the least of these brothers and sisters of mine, you did for me'" (Matthew 25:37, 39 – 40).

He wasn't in Romania for Joni's sake alone. He wasn't there just because they were getting married and he needed to learn the ropes about all this travel stuff.

He was there because Jesus wanted him there.

The thought sobered him. He, Ken Tada, history teacher and football coach, had a job to do. And whatever their team was able to do to encourage the oppressed believers in that place, to look into the plight of orphans and the disabled, "the least of these brothers and sisters of mine," would be a direct service to Jesus Himself. And He would take note of it.

According to the government, however, there were no disabled people.

In Ceauşescu's workers' paradise, everyone was able-bodied and whole ... or so their government guides informed them.

Their official tour of the country's few "rehabilitation centers" seemed to bear out the government line; they were practically empty. Told that they would be taken to a "school for the rehabilitation of children," they were escorted into a roomful of unsmiling teenagers dressed in blue uniforms and sitting erect and silent at their desks. On cue, one boy dutifully showed them his leg brace, another her amputated arm. *These were the disabled? Seriously?*

At another so-called facility for people with disabilities, they toured dim hallways lit by a few hanging lightbulbs. In one of the many white-tiled rooms, the official showed them a few prosthetic legs and braces. But where were the people? Where were the wheelchairs?

Toward the end of the visit, a few disabled people were ushered into the hallway to meet the "Western visitors." One man was in a vintage wheelchair, and several others hobbled along on crutches. Joni tried to strike up a cheerful conversation with them, but they replied in tight monosyllables, their faces as blank as the white-tiled walls. *They're afraid*, Joni thought. *Scared to death. And they can't wait for us to get out of here.*

As they drove in silence back to the hotel, Joni remembered studying about the Soviet Empire in her Modern and Contemporary History class in high school. She recalled being afraid of the "people behind the Iron Curtain," as if they were of a different race — stalwart and strong like those imposing Leninist sculptures of farmers holding sickles and workers wielding hammers. She had felt sure that, given the chance, they were ready to storm across the borders and overpower the West.

But none of the citizens she had seen so far looked anything like the statues or the propaganda photos. They didn't look stalwart and strong; they just looked afraid.

e⁀

Pastor Sarac prayed the blessing over their dinner but seemed in a hurry from the first bite.

Two elderly women dressed in long skirts and wearing babushkas bustled in and out of the kitchen with steaming platters of garlic chicken, sausage, and onions. Joni later learned that these women and several others from the church had taken turns standing in long food lines to make sure they got two chickens and some onions for their American guests.

Wind-driven rain spattered against the windows as they ate.

After what seemed no longer than ten minutes, the pastor pushed back from the table, wiping his hand on a napkin. "We must hurry to get into the church," he said.

Surprised, Joni glanced at a clock. "But the service doesn't begin until nine o'clock," she said. "It's early yet."

Pastor Sarac flashed a quick, nervous smile. "Oh … I do not think so, dear sister."

Leaving the pastor's apartment and stepping out into the

night, they were stunned at the sight before them. Rain was pelting down on a sea of people lined up in the darkness. Clogging the path to the church entrance were elderly men huddled beside their wives, young mothers holding babies, fathers clasping the hands of their children — and all of them seemingly oblivious to the soaking rain, smiling and staring wide-eyed at Joni in her wheelchair.

Jay and Judy shook hands vigorously with everyone and kept insisting, "Thank you, yes; please, let's go *inside* the church."

The crowds cleared a path for Joni's wheelchair, but no one else could enter because the church was already packed. Ken and Joni looked around the auditorium in wonder. Elderly people crowded each pew, while younger ones stood in the aisles, shoulder to shoulder, three abreast, in row after row up the middle aisle. Up the stairs to the balcony, the kids were jammed like sardines, and the upper section appeared to sag from the weight of many more. The air was hot and steamy and smelled of wet garments — and flowers. When Joni glanced to see if the windows could be opened a little, she found herself looking into the smiling faces of young children and teenagers sitting on each and every sill. Behind them, even more people stood outside in the rain, jostling to get a view.

Ken had never imagined such a scene, and it was still difficult to comprehend that he was a part of it all. These people — even if they spoke a different language, followed unfamiliar customs, and lived in circumstances wildly different from his own — were his brothers and sisters in Jesus. He couldn't shake the thought that he had more in common, much closer ties, to these Christian strangers than he had with his non-Christian next-door neighbors in his Burbank condo.

Pastor Sarac said a few words of introduction in Romanian, one of the most beautiful languages Joni had ever heard. Someone had described it to her as "a blend of strong, confident Slavic tempered with the passionate, rhythmic flow of a Romance language, complete with the rolling *r*'s!" When the pastor led the assembly in a hymn, the music was simply stunning. Sweet and strong, robust and wrung from the deep places of the soul. It had all the passion and suppressed Slavonic longing of a Dvořák melody, but ran deeper still.

Tears filled Joni's eyes. *This was the song of the persecuted church.*

Seven years later, a peaceful protest around a pastor's home in Timișoara would help launch the Romanian revolution.

After the introductions, Ken wheeled Joni's chair to the front, and she turned to face the crowd for the first time. Immediately, women and children surged forward with bouquets of flowers, placing them in her lap and all around her wheelchair. And there to her left and to her right, on the floor between the pews and the platform, were people with disabilities. Some lay on thin mattresses and mats or sat in homemade wheelchairs constructed of bicycle parts ... the blind and the deaf, the lame and the mentally challenged, men and women with twisted legs and spines. She recognized those with polio, spina bifida, and cerebral palsy, all straining to see their American counterpart. And how many more, huddled in sodden coats, hats, and blankets outside in the rain, were hoping to hear something, see something, that might bring a little hope into their dreary lives?

Yes, Romania had its disabled population, all right. They had simply been shunned and hidden away in back rooms, attics, and basements; frowned at and despised in public; forbidden to ever enter a hotel, restaurant, or market — their very existence denied by a megalomaniac dictator.

That night in the hotel, Judy and Jay unloaded pockets and purses stuffed with tightly folded pieces of paper, piling them on the bed. Ken and Joni had been given notes too, which they added to the growing heap. They sat up that night reading many of them, desperate stories of people, all pleading in halting English for hope or help. A few asked for knowledge of medical cures for "our mongoloid child" or spinal cord injury or stroke or psychotic problems. One said, "Can you help my son who is a spastic?" Another note read: "My daughter needs a wheelchair, please?"

After a while, and without words, the four of them looked at each other, the same thought occurring to all of them. *Maybe we can do some good here — return with wheelchairs and crutches... perhaps bring Bibles or my books in the Romanian language... could this be why God brought us here?*

At that time, few people in the West knew anything about the hidden population of disabled men, women, and children in Ceauşescu's Romania. But now ... they all felt as if a mantle had been laid on their shoulders, a burden of responsibility they could not, and would not, ignore.

God had not forgotten His most vulnerable children in this beleaguered land. When Jesus addressed His letter to Pergamum in the book of Revelation, He might as well have been speaking of the Christians in Romania: "I know where you live — where Satan has his throne. Yet you remain true to my name" (Revelation 2:13).

Now He had brought them there, Ken and Joni, Jay and Judy, and they had looked into the eyes of Romania's suffering believers.

They wouldn't forget.

And somehow, they would be back.

⌒

Next stop, Poland. It might have been a tightly controlled Communist state with its own cadre of secret police, but compared to the dark, nearly demonic oppression of Romania, it felt almost light and airy.

Joni spoke before churches in towns with names like Katowice and Wrocław, and together they presented the gospel of Jesus Christ to disabled people at rehabilitation centers.

At one church, noisy and packed to capacity, Ken and Joni prayed together behind a flimsy wooden screen before rolling out in front of the crowded pews. He gripped her lifeless fingers, praying that the Holy Spirit would speak through them to the curious, excited, and eager men, women, and children who filled the auditorium to capacity.

She had been in similar places on similar nights in different parts of the world, but tonight was different. Tonight, Ken was there. Her husband-to-be. It wasn't just Joni; it was Ken and Joni. And as they prayed together, she felt a new strength and confidence. For Ken, it was yet another glimpse into the future. *So this is what it will be like…*

Joni peeked out from behind the screen into the faces of the people of Poland. Farmers with their families. Steelworkers and miners. Little boys who tugged at each other and bumped one another's shoulders. Young women with brightly colored kerchiefs, spots of blue and red and yellow dotted throughout a crowd dressed mostly in heavy dark coats and sweaters.

Two older women squeezed together on the front pew, their heads thinly framed in tight black scarves. For an instant, she saw them as she might have painted them, with faces lined and weary, yet full rosy cheeks and sparkling blue eyes. They were looking expectantly at their pastor, as did everyone else, whether jammed into the pews or standing in the middle and side aisles, listening to his introductory remarks.

It seemed so loud that night, even though no one but the pastor was talking. It occurred to Joni that the din was from hundreds of coats, scarves, shoes, canes, and crutches crowding and rustling against one another. The cold plaster walls of the church echoed the sound off the high wooden ceiling. It was a chilly night outside, yet in the church the air was tight, hot, and humid. And charged with excitement.

A young man, probably afflicted with some form of multiple sclerosis, sat humped over in his pea jacket, his hands twisting a handkerchief. His wheelchair was very, very old, the drab green leather worn and torn. The wheels were different sizes, as though he had pieced together mismatching parts, perhaps cannibalizing foot pedals and armrests from other, even older chairs.

The bright, scrubbed face of a young girl looked on, her lips full, naturally pink, and parted in a mild and gentle smile. Joni pointed her out to Ken. "Look at her eyes!" she said. Ken nodded. Her eyes were absolutely glowing. "She knows Jesus," Joni said. "I'm sure of it." She was sitting in a molded orange plastic chair someone had placed at the end of the first pew and leaned on a black cane. Her spindly thin calves were encased in old leg braces — probably a polio survivor.

Joni couldn't help but glance down at her own wheelchair, each aluminum spoke gleaming and clean, her seat outfitted with an expensive black cushion. She had already met many people with disabilities in Poland who sat on old couch cushions in their wheelchairs, or perhaps doubled-up feather pillows. She felt like she was about to drive a shiny new Mercedes into a street filled with ancient Pontiacs and battered Studebakers. She was suddenly very glad she had worn a plain woolen sweater that night, and that her hair had been simply styled. The last thing she wanted to look like in front of these people was glamorous. Without even thinking about it, she began to rub the blush off her cheeks with her sweater sleeve.

Guessing what she was thinking, Ken reached around her neck, tilted her head back, and kissed her. It was reassurance like no one else could have given her in that moment. How glad she was to have him there with her!

In the next moment, he wheeled her onto the platform and parked her chair next to the woman who would translate their message. The noise in the church increased as people slid forward in their seats or jostled in the aisles to get a better view.

Ken was still in awe of Joni's fame. Here they were in Communist Poland, and many of these people had seen her movie or read her books in Polish. And now ... here he was at her side, and part of that picture. In his younger years, he would have never imagined such a thing. You just never knew what life would bring when you surrendered it to serving the Lord.

Joni and Ken traded shy, nervous smiles with the audience, and then he walked off the platform. She began to speak, finding her cadence with the translator. Love, concern, and joy seemed to radiate from her in waves. What an amazing gift she had with an audience! He could see her enthusiasm reflected in the faces looking on intently. They were warmed by her, encouraged just to be near her. A wizened old woman in a front pew nodded and smiled, drinking in every word. The young disabled girl in the orange chair leaned forward on her cane, smiling with confidence and hope.

After Joni's message, Ken rejoined her on the platform and began speaking about their upcoming marriage, with its challenges and joys. *Having a translator isn't a bad experience*, he told himself. It gave him time to collect his thoughts a little.

Ken quoted 2 Corinthians 12:9 – 10, relating how Joni's disability had become a weakness about which to boast, allowing God's power to rest on their lives. He had used those words before, but on that night in Poland, they seemed almost electric with meaning, and he watched, or sensed, people nodding their heads in acknowledgment.

As he spoke, Joni thought to herself, *But they mustn't think of us as extraordinary or heroic. They mustn't think of me that way —a celebrity from the West with wings on her wheelchair who smiles and paints and writes and sings. I must find a way to tell them more clearly how we struggle with so many things and fall short so often, just as they do.*

For that night, however, it was enough that they had brought words of blessing and hope from a distant America — and a Savior who wasn't distant at all.

⁓

Since both Ken and Joni were history buffs and interested in events surrounding World War II, they took advantage of the opportunity to visit the site of a Nazi concentration camp — Auschwitz-Birkenau — in Poland.

It ended up being a more jarring experience than either of

them had anticipated. What stuck in Joni's mind in years to come, however, were the wildflowers.

In Auschwitz, at the site and around the museum, and in Birkenau, where the evidence of the camp had fallen away, the grounds were carpeted with tiny white daisies. There seemed to be untold thousands of them, poking up through the new spring grass, nodding delicate heads in the breezes.

"Do you suppose the government plants them?" Joni whispered to Ken, out of earshot from their Polish hosts, who were guiding them.

Ken shook his head. "I don't know. Maybe not. Maybe God planted them. Anything bright helps in this place."

In spite of the wildflowers and the intervening years, Auschwitz was a chilling, depressing place.

Joni noticed a row of lovely rose bushes planted just yards away from the gas chambers. Obviously, *those* had been planted. Their guide nodded yes, observing that there had certainly been no flowers when Auschwitz was in operation. Every wildflower, every blade of grass, was plucked clean, right down to the naked clay, by starving prisoners. They ate everything that grew, trying to stay alive.

To Joni, the carpet of daisies seemed like a covering of God's grace over a scene of inconceivable horror ... or perhaps a memorial.

Inside the museum, one of the first displays was housed in a large room behind glass, filled with piles and piles of prosthetic legs, walkers, crutches, canes, and everything else that any person with a disability might have had when he or she had come to that place.

The disabled were always the first to die.

Years later, Joni would learn that when Nazi "medical" teams across the Third Reich began doing their gruesome experiments on "low value" people, they began by pulling people with mental and physical problems out of various institutions and carting them off in the night to their laboratories. But not just anyone.

At least initially they only chose people who had no visitors, no family or friends coming to see them. The Nazis reasoned that people without advocates were easy marks because no one would notice or care if they went missing. Disabled people like Joni had been labeled as "useless bread gobblers."

How incredibly sad, she had thought. And she felt an overwhelming sense of gratitude for her family, and especially for Ken, her husband-to-be. *I have an advocate*, she thought. *Someone who will be there for me and stand up for me, no matter what.* For the rest of her life, as long as Ken lived, she had an advocate, a champion ... and a friend.

Auschwitz contained every horror she had ever read about. Bare bricks and barbed wire ... storehouses of eyeglasses and gold teeth, canes and crutches, shoes, hearing aids ... stacks of yellowed and dusty record books bearing neatly inscribed names ... gallows and guard towers ... even the ominous chimneys and the ovens.

But she hadn't expected the flowers. The tiny little wisps of white innocence, carpeting the grounds.

They journeyed the short distance from Auschwitz to Birkenau. Here, trainloads of Jews and dissidents had been emptied out into the freezing night to face the machine guns of pitiless and soul-dead men. Children were gun-butted one way; their mothers herded the other. Men were separated into groups of the old and young. But virtually all of them, millions of them, ended up in one place — the incinerator, now crumbled and overgrown — at the end of the camp.

Nothing was left standing at Birkenau. Their hosts explained that what appeared to be orderly rows of heaps of brick were once the smokestacks of wooden barracks. Nothing remained of the guard towers. Even the train tracks and railroad ties were gone, uprooted or simply moldered away.

Joni shivered, but not from the cold. The camps were stark reminders that wherever Satan ruled in the world, people weren't valued as those who bear the stamp of God's image. Only "useful," able-bodied lives had any value. The message of the Nazis — and Ceaușescu's Romania — was that "you are better off dead than disabled. We don't need people like you."

But Ken needed her.

How wonderful to be needed. Wanted. Cherished. Loved for something more than physical "usefulness."

She dropped her gaze to the daisies Ken had tucked into the straps of her arm splints. And smiled. *Her advocate.*

The children of their Polish hosts had remained in the van during the tours of the death camps, absorbed in playing Mario Bros. games on their Nintendos. It made Ken, the teacher, thoughtful. Was that the attitude of the coming generation? Absorbed in the latest gadget coming out of the West, with no interest in learning about the terrible historical events that occurred only miles from where they lived? How quickly would the terrible lessons of history fade?

 ℯ

In Athens, just before flying home, they had been invited to attend the Greek premiere of the *Joni* movie.

Organizers of the event sent a big black Mercedes to pick them up at the hotel. At the theater, a large group of Joni admirers crowded around the car as the driver and Ken fetched her wheelchair from the trunk. Ken was dazed by the spotlight, flashbulbs, and the excited murmur of the crowd. *I can't believe this*, he told himself. *I'm marrying a movie star. Where's the red carpet?* He lifted her out of the car, and Joni emerged, smiling and waving to the friendly crowd, just as if she'd done it a million times before. As they picked her up, however, the clamp on her leg bag broke, releasing its contents on the sidewalk.

Well, well, Joni thought to herself, *I must have been letting this international movie premiere thing go to my head a little. Thanks, Father, for helping me keep things in perspective!*

Before they left town, everyone wanted to see the Parthenon, and no one really imagined it would be wheelchair accessible!

Ken's weight training, however, combined with a good dose of a history teacher's excited adrenaline, enabled him to carry Joni all 150 steps to the magnificent ruins at the crown of the Acropolis.

There, late in the afternoon, Ken held his bride-to-be, looking out over Athens and the Aegean Sea and Sea of Crete in the misty distance. What a trip this had been! How could he ever look at life in the same way again?

They looked out as far as they could see in all directions. If you stayed there long enough, lingering from sunset to moonrise, you could watch the columns of the Parthenon turn from beige to golden to rose to stark white.

Maybe so ... but Ken was ready to find a restaurant and order a plate of sizzling *soutzoukakia*.

Carrying fiancées up hilltops was hungry work.

CHAPTER FIVE

AT THE ALTAR

*Never be afraid to trust
an unknown future to a known God.*
CORRIE TEN BOOM

JUNE 15, 1982

In the days before their wedding, Joni saw all that a bride-to-be would hope to see in the eyes of her groom.

Love. Longing. Quiet strength. Nervous excitement. Sheer joy. But she also saw something else, something that concerned her.

Ken *idealized* her.

He had a bright, shining image of her in his mind, and he'd had it since he first saw her in person at the Young Life banquet in Burbank. He'd told her how he'd wanted to meet her and talk to her that night but hadn't had a chance with all the people crowding around. He had read her biographies (*Joni* and *A Step Further*), watched her in televised Billy Graham crusades, and had just recently seen her movie.

She understood the "Joni persona thing," and how that tended to skew people's perceptions of her. Because of what she had been through in life and how she had endured it, people wanted to make her into Saint Joni. This was the legendary young woman who always smiled and bravely faced any crisis with triumphant faith, the one whose wheelchair hovered just a few inches above the ground as she sailed through life. This was in spite of the fact that in her books and devotionals she had tried hard to poke holes in that inflated, bigger-than-life image. She had done her best to be authentic and transparent, to show people that she was a sinner, that she dealt with pride, pettiness, lust, jealousy, and anger — just like everyone else on the planet.

Yes, part of her enjoyed the attention, the spotlight, and the affirmation. But mostly, she just felt vertigo up on a high pedestal. And there had been times when she deliberately toppled herself off that high platform just so she could be back on the same level with everyone else.

Nevertheless, she couldn't help being Joni. And she couldn't deny the wondrous things God had done for her and enabled her to do. Like the prophet Samuel in the Old Testament, she had raised her Ebenezer, her "stone of help," declaring to all, "Thus far the LORD has helped me." She couldn't walk away from the role He had given her: to be an encourager and cheerleader for people with disabilities, as well as for the discouraged and disenfranchised.

She had come to accept it and live with it as a matter of course; it went with the territory. But she had worried about Ken sometimes. Was he marrying the persona or the real person? It felt at times like he was walking into marriage with an idyllic view of who she was and what a lifetime with a quadriplegic woman really meant.

Was he really ready for it? *All* of it? He had to be, or it wouldn't be right to go forward with it. It wouldn't be fair to either one of them.

She remembered a conversation they'd had back when they were dating. On a chilly night, they had just emerged from her van and faced one another in the darkness of her open garage.

"Ken," she had been saying, "I'm afraid you don't know me. I'm afraid you have me built up in your mind — like one of those plaster of Paris saints."

She turned her chair so she could face him squarely. With the bright moonlight behind her, however, she cast a shadow over his face and couldn't see his features.

"I feel like I know the real you," he said. "All I need to know."

"You *don't* know me. You know a book. A movie. A record album. You take me to all these speaking engagements where I have to look my best, speak my best, and be at my best in front of everybody. You see me after some very gifted women have labored for hours over my hair and my makeup and my clothing. But life can't be all 'best.' There are things about me that you wouldn't like at all. Things that might turn your stomach."

He didn't speak ... and she couldn't see his face.

She went on. "I'm not just talking about the bathroom stuff — leg bags and all the rest of it that goes with being paralyzed. There are things about me, my personality — times when I'm not very nice to be around. I can be selfish. I can be a perfectionist."

"So what are you saying?" he stepped out of her shadow, showing his face in the moonlight. A strong, kind, honest face. He loved her; she could see that. And at that moment he was also troubled. So was she.

"I don't know ... I don't know," she said.

She just wanted him to be *sure*. Sure of who she was. Sure of what he was signing up for. If he was just starstruck and in love with an image, how would that get them through the long years ahead, dealing with the myriad complications of her disability? Did he understand she had a limited life expectancy? Had he really grappled with how difficult it would be, unless God healed her? Did he have perspective? Had he been able at all to look down through the years at what this would mean for his life? His mother had been troubled when she met Joni. Confused. It wasn't what she had wanted for her only son. Maybe he should have listened to her genuine, heartfelt concerns.

Ken had always said yes, he understood. That he got it. That God was in this. That he had counted the cost and wanted to go forward anyway.

She could only pray it was true.

JULY 3, 1982

She drove to the church with her sister Kathy in the van, negotiating the traffic of the Ventura Freeway, sailing along in her preferred middle lane. It seemed like any other day in L.A.

But it wasn't.

All those cars and trucks speeding behind, ahead, and on both sides of her had no idea what a landmark day — a day of days! — this really was. So she and her sister began singing out loud, "I'm getting married in the morning! Ding dong! The bells are gonna chime!" Joni capped the song with a shout in her van. *"It's my wedding day!"*

Grace Community Church was big enough to have its own bridal salon, and that's where Joni got ready. The preparation began with her girlfriends lying her down on a couch and shifting her paralyzed body this way and that so they could pull her wedding gown over her. After she was corseted and buttoned, they lifted her back into her wheelchair, draping her gown carefully over a thin wire mesh that covered the wheels to keep the fabric from getting caught in the spokes. She watched in the mirror as they combed her hair and applied her makeup. She was being "prepared as a bride adorned for her husband," as it said in the Scriptures, and it was through the willing hands of others. It seemed a little surreal to just sit there and watch herself becoming a bride.

Everyone else, it seemed, was scurrying around, chattering, doing this and that, while she sat stationary in the middle of it all, a still point in a turning world. The fact was, even though she couldn't scurry around if she wanted to, she felt calm and peaceful.

When the organ music began down in the auditorium, she wheeled herself toward the salon door, pausing for a moment in front of a full-length mirror. Somehow, sitting in the midst of all the fabric and covered wheels, she felt like a float in the Rose Parade. Maybe she should try that signature Rose Parade wave the beauty queens used from their perches in those long, white Lincoln limo convertibles.

An usher brought word that all the guests had been seated, and it was time to line up. They moved across the deserted grounds to the sanctuary entrance. At that last moment, Joni had wanted desperately to rearrange the disorderly bouquet of daisies in her lap, but couldn't do it. She had elected not to wear her arm splints, and that made it impossible to adjust *anything*. It was all she could do to steer her power chair.

Someone cracked open the door to the auditorium, and the majestic organ music swirled around them, stirring them. Way up front, she caught a glimpse of her longtime friend Steve Estes, who was helping officiate the wedding, standing with her pastor, John MacArthur. Even then, the sense of calm remained. She thought to herself, *I've been more nervous speaking in front of churches half this size.*

There was her daddy, stepping through the door to escort her, cutting quite a dashing figure in his gray morning suit and Windsor cravat. But he would have looked wonderful to her if he'd been wearing his usual attire of suspendered jeans and a flannel shirt. He beamed at her, the pride shining in his eyes. She was his youngest daughter, and his namesake. He smiled at her as if to say, *You're not my little pal anymore, not my cowgirl. And I'm glad!*

She motioned to him with her head, and he bent down so she could speak into his ear, above the organ music. "I'll go slow, so you can keep up with me!" He nodded, handing off one of his crutches to Judy and holding on to the armrest of her chair for support.

"Nervous?" he asked.

She smiled, shaking her head no, still feeling swathed in an unusual sense of calm.

"You're marrying a good one, honey girl."

Yes, she was!

As the last bridesmaid began to walk down the aisle, Joni

inched her chair closer to the door, peering through the crack to see if she could catch a glimpse of Ken. Then she glanced down at her gown ... and groaned aloud. *Oh no!* She had somehow managed to wheel over the hem, leaving a large greasy tire mark — an awful black tread on her white gown! Everyone had tried so hard, but as she looked down at her dress, it hung clumpy and uneven. Even though her chair had been spiffed up for the occasion it looked big as a Buick, with wheels and gears still visible through the wire mesh. And then there were those poor daisies, the bouquet lying off center in her lap, looking as if it had been thrown there.

She wasn't a picture-perfect bride by any stretch. Did Ken realize that? Suddenly the old worry punctured her pre-ceremony calm. Did he see her for who she really was, or was he still looking through some rose-hued prism? How she hated those grease marks! They invariably reminded her of stains on her own soul. She had often wondered, even after all God had accomplished through her life over the years, *Does Christ see anything lovely in me?* Yes, she had been justified before God — she knew that — but she was so far, so very far, from what He wanted her to be. She felt unworthy. And especially now, sitting at the beginning of the aisle, clad in gleaming white.

There were her friends from the office. From her Bible study group. And there was ...

And then she saw him, waiting at attention with hands clasped behind him, looking tall and stately in his morning suit. But he, too, was craning his head, just like she was, peering down the aisle, looking for her.

Suddenly, in an instant, all the worry and self-loathing washed away. *He was looking for her. Watching for her. Waiting for her. His bride.* Her face suddenly grew hot, and her heart pounded in her chest. She had seen her beloved, and wells of emotion broke loose. Joy. Anticipation. An overwhelming longing to be with him. If only she could get up out of that chair and run to him, that good, kind, strong, ordinary-extraordinary man who loved her. Who wanted her.

The music crescendoed, and Joni and her dad began their arduous journey down the aisle, one hobbled by arthritis and the other paralyzed in a wheelchair.

In a strange moment of almost dual vision, Joni saw Ken the bridegroom and Jesus the Bridegroom at the same time. *This is how it will be when we see Jesus. Overcome with longing. Overtaken with joy. We'll catch a glimpse of Him and want to run to Him. Right out of this life and into the next one.*

There was no way, even with rehearsals and programs, even having attended scores of weddings, she could have prepared herself for this. How she looked no longer mattered to her. She forgot all about the tire marks, the dispirited daisies, the clunky wheelchair, and the clumpy dress. In that moment, she didn't feel ugly or unworthy. The love in Ken's eyes, so intense it was almost hard to look at, washed it all away. In his eyes, she was the pure and perfect bride. His bride. That's what he saw, and that's what changed her.

⁊

On the way to the airport, she asked him if he had seen what a mess she had been. Had he noticed the tire marks, the grease stain, the disheveled daisies, and the way her gown had bunched up?

"No," he said, shaking his head. "I thought you were gorgeous."

Gorgeous. He had dismissed it all with a word — all her anxieties, regrets, and secret sorrows. He hadn't seen a thing but his lovely bride. She had to laugh at herself in that moment, even if not out loud. The most beautiful parallels were shining in her mind as she thought of that first moment in heaven when she would see God's Son. One look at His face, and all the worries and fears, all the disappointments and sadness of a lifetime lived in a broken world, would fade. Flee like darkness from a room when someone flips on a light. All the disgusting stains of earthly life would be purified away, dissolved by one look from the Bridegroom's eyes. And in that day, too, her face would flush, her heart would pound, and it would all be more beautiful and joyful than she could have imagined in a million years.

For now, however, she had an earthly bridegroom to feel happy about.

And a honeymoon!

ॐ

Ken carried her over the threshold of the 747 bound for Hawaii.

The flight attendants directed them to the first row of seats, away from the view of the few other passengers in first class.

Honeymooners. A silly word. And with all the special treatment — a surprise cake, Hawaiian leis, orange juice served in crystal glasses on a silver tray — everyone on board must have known it was their first full day as a married couple.

They snuggled into their seats, savoring the illusion of privacy, and rubbed noses and laughed. Ken had wondered if it would feel strange to be married, but it hadn't felt strange at all. It felt like the most natural thing in the world.

They'd had a little talk the night before, acknowledging to each other that it wouldn't be easy. Quadriplegia wasn't easy. Even on a good day, it was difficult and challenging. And yes, there would be disappointments and heartaches and those inevitable times when one or both of them would wish, *If only we could be "normal," even for one night, even for one afternoon.* There would be times when what they believed in their hearts and their heads would be challenged by the raw reality of trying to flesh it all out, with what might be diminished resources.

But this was their honeymoon, and God was smiling down at them. Ken lifted the glass of juice to Joni's mouth and twined her fingers in his. In her mind, she could almost feel his hand, or at least remember what holding hands felt like. They shared secrets and told each other how wonderful their first night together had been.

"We're ready to begin the movie."

A flight attendant bent over Joni and closed her window shade. Ken pushed their seats back, slipped the headphones over her head, and stuffed a pillow in between them.

The cabin darkened, and the name of the movie flashed across their small viewing screen. *Whose Life Is It Anyway?*

"Oh no," Joni groaned.

"What? Have you seen it?"

"No, but I know what it's about," she whispered. "Richard Dreyfuss plays a guy who gets his neck broken, becomes despondent, and argues with the hospital staff and his family to let him die."

"Oh ... well, that sounds like a lot of fun."

"It's pretty depressing stuff."

A suddenly embarrassed flight attendant knelt beside their seats and began to apologize profusely. "And here it is your honeymoon! Of all the movies. Oh my gosh, I can't believe this."

After she left, they grinned at each other, slipped off the headphones, and tuned out the movie. Anyway, who was despondent about being paralyzed? Not them! The Richard Dreyfuss movie was all about an obsession with death. But this would be a week that was all about life. A new life together, a life the Father Himself had planned for them before the beginning of time. Hollywood didn't have a clue how that could work, but it didn't matter. They didn't need Hollywood's approval.

The five-hour flight passed quickly, even without the movie, and they arrived at their gate in Honolulu. Judy and Rana, a longtime friend and assistant, came down from their seats on the 747's upper deck to help Joni get off the plane. Yes, this honeymoon would be a little different from the norm, with two helpers who had come along with them — women who would appear when needed and discreetly disappear just as quickly. Someone needed to teach Ken how to do everything, from giving Joni a bath to getting her dressed. The helpers would stay at their own hotel several blocks from the newlyweds, enjoying their own vacation.

Clothes changed and out on the beach, Ken kicked off his flip-flops, ran both hands through his thatch of thick black hair, clasped them behind his head, yawned, and stretched. The tails of his Hawaiian print shirt fluttered in the soft trade wind.

He definitely looked Hawaiian now. Every inch the handsome "island guy" she had spotted in Grace Community Church once upon a time.

With Joni parked on the Waikiki walkway in the sun, Ken walked down to the surf to stick his toes in the water.

"George, look who it is! It's *Joanie*! I don't believe this!"

Joni glanced up the sidewalk to see a family of three approaching. Did she know them? No … but they knew her! Through the years, she had experienced this time and again. People would recognize her from her books or her movie, and they'd approach her like they were old friends. It was understandable, and for Joni, no big deal. But this was different. She was on her honeymoon.

Ken, evidently delighted with the warmth of the surf, had waded out up to his knees.

"Well, I'll be," said George, reaching for his camera in his ABC Stores Aloha tote bag. "I'll get a snapshot!"

Joni didn't want her picture taken. Not then. But apparently, they couldn't conceive of that. Or didn't care. Sighing, she made an effort to smile at them and ask their names. Their son, in a bright red South Carolina Fighting Gamecocks T-shirt, stuck his hands in his pockets and looked away, apparently embarrassed by his parents accosting this stranger in a wheelchair.

"Oh, honey!" The woman in the brightly colored muumuu reached around Joni's shoulder and pulled her toward her, squeezing her cheek against Joni's. "We're just so *thrilled* to meet you. We read your book and saw your movie, and my neighbors just aren't going to *believe* this when we get home!"

"Hold still," George commanded, waving his hand and staring through his camera's viewfinder. "And Junior, get in the picture."

"Please …" Joni protested. "I'd rather you didn't."

At this their faces fell. Stunned into momentary silence, they couldn't believe what they were hearing. *Not take a picture?*

"You see," Joni said in a low voice, "it's my honeymoon" — as if sharing a secret.

"You're *married*?" The woman, still holding Joni by the shoulders, pulled back to look at her from arm's length. "Why, isn't that wonderful! It's wonderful, isn't it, George?"

George, still disappointed over not getting a picture, mumbled something.

"Who is the lucky fellow?" She looked around for someone who might be Joni's husband, ignoring the dark Asian man who approached in his Hawaiian shirt, shorts, and flip-flops.

The man and woman, who had evidently taken Ken for a Hawaiian tour guide, appeared just a little shocked when he stopped behind Joni's wheelchair and leaned over to give her a warm, affectionate, and very proprietary hug.

"This is my husband," Joni said proudly. "Ken Tada." As she spoke, it struck her that this was one of the first times she'd had to introduce him in that way.

But suddenly the little meeting seemed more awkward than ever. Were they expecting someone different? Maybe someone … white?

"Oh … well, yes, hello." The woman hiked her tote bag on her shoulder and extended her hand. Her husband did the same. "Pleased to meet you, Mr. Eareckson," he said.

Finally, they said their farewells, and the family walked on down the beach.

"They evidently don't approve of me," Ken said, pushing Joni's chair back toward the hotel.

"And who cares what *they* think?" Joni replied.

"*Mr. Eareckson!* Tell me, do I look Swedish?"

He sounded hurt. "I'm sorry, Ken. That's — that's the way people are sometimes. They don't even consider if it's rude or not." She couldn't get around the fact that she had become a recognizable public person. Was Ken ready for that? Ready to be ignored by excited people who wanted a photo opportunity with Joni but weren't really interested in *him*?

She felt protective of him, defensive for him. Sometimes the spotlight that people shone on her cast a long shadow over anyone who stood beside her wheelchair.

This public aspect of life wouldn't be easy for either of them.

For that matter, the private part wouldn't be a piece of cake either.

e

If Ken and Joni had held different views on marriage and hadn't been so insistent on honoring God right from the beginning, they might have gone off somewhere together before they were married to "try out" a few things, just to see how it worked.

But they didn't do that.

Their honeymoon was a true honeymoon of discovery, and part of that discovery for Ken meant learning all of Joni's routines, including her toileting routines.

They had talked about it, of course. Joni had done her best to walk him through her day and the handling of all the daily necessities. But talking about such private things in low casual voices while sipping lemonade at an outdoor café in Southern California wasn't the same as actually being "hands-on."

On the second night of their honeymoon, Ken carried Joni to the toilet for her bowel routine. And it was a little messy. Ken was expressionless, helpful, and kind, but Joni felt a little surge of fear well up in her heart. Here they were, barely forty-eight hours past their wedding vows, and Ken was having to lift her onto a toilet and take care of the cleanup job.

Oh, God, she prayed, *I hope he's prepared for this.*

He wasn't.

As much as he had tried to reason it all through, talk it all through, and pray it all through, he wasn't prepared for how *profound* her disability truly was. Actually seeing her so — so helpless was a shock. It shouldn't have been, but it was.

Joni always handled everything so well and with such grace that people tended to forget she was paralyzed below the neck! She had always seemed so much larger than life to him — so beautiful, so poised, so radiant in her faith, so skillful in her speaking and singing and painting and meeting people in public. How could he *not* have an idealized image of her persona? For goodness' sake, this was Joni Eareckson, whose first book had sold millions, someone who was recognized by Christians around the world.

But now she was Joni Eareckson *Tada*.

She would always have an adoring public, but she belonged to Ken Tada. She depended on Ken Tada.

Was he up to that task ... *for the rest of their lives together?*

It took a while to separate himself emotionally from what happened in the bathroom, but he was able to shake it off. With God's help, he believed he was up to the task. She believed he was too.

But it didn't take away the fear.

APRIL 1983

They moved away from the graveside of their friend Corrie ten Boom under a sun-splashed canopy of new green leaves. Neither of them spoke as they reflected on this gentle, courageous woman's remarkable life. She had passed away on April 15, on her ninety-first birthday. At the memorial service, the pastor related how before Corrie's passing she had specifically instructed him not to speak about *her*, but rather about the love of Jesus.

And so he had.

It had been the same every time Joni had visited with Corrie: Jesus was always at the center of her thoughts and words. She rarely spoke of "the Christian walk" or "the Christian experience." She didn't speak of Christ as though He were some creed, doctrine, or even lifestyle. She spoke about a Person. Someone she loved more than anyone or anything else in all the world.

It was the same during their last visit in her home, though her speech had been limited by a series of crippling strokes.

Joni finally broke their thoughtful silence. "Corrie's life reminds me of that Scripture in Corinthians, where Paul says he didn't come to them with eloquence or all this wisdom or beautiful words. Remember? He said, 'I resolved to know nothing while I was with you except Jesus Christ and him crucified.'"[10]

The fine gravel crunched under the wheels of Joni's chair, and a breeze whispered through the new leaves, rustling Ken's thick black hair.

"How is it," she said, "that we get so caught up in explaining our walk in Christ, our life in Christ, or some spiritual experience instead of simply talking about *Him*?"

Ken nodded. Jesus — the real, living Person of Jesus — had meant so much to both of them. He had pulled Ken out of some frightening pits as a young man in college; He had walked with Joni through those dark and heartbreaking years of learning to accept the unacceptable: that she would be paralyzed for life. And against all the odds, He had brought them together as husband and wife, that they might serve Him better as a team than as individuals.

Was there a danger as they "settled into" married life of nudging Jesus into the background just a little? How terrible that would be! Would He, could He, ever become some abstract doctrine or generic "way of life" to them? Would they love Him as much as a couple as they had loved Him and delighted in Him and depended on Him as Christian singles?

Passing by the gravestones of Fairhaven Memorial Park in Santa Ana, it was something to think about.

This life, *their* life, was too short to let themselves become distracted from *the* Life.

Suddenly the irony dawned on her. Tante Corrie was gone now ... and they were leaving her graveside. But here she was again, still teaching Joni's heart.

And that made Joni smile.

CHAPTER SIX

THE TESTING YEARS

I'm feeling terrible — I couldn't feel worse!...
Help me understand these things inside and out
  so I can ponder your miracle-wonders.
My sad life's dilapidated, a falling-down barn;
  build me up again by your Word ...
I grasp and cling to whatever you tell me;
  GOD, don't let me down!
I'll run the course you lay out for me
  if you'll just show me how.

PSALM 119:25, 27 – 28, 31 – 32 MSG

Misty mornings in London ... spring twilights in Paris ... a family dinner and golden sunset in the hills of Transylvania ... gazing out across the Aegean from the Parthenon ... seeking out the disabled in the garbage dumps of Manila ... heading behind the Iron Curtain where intrigue, mystery, and danger held sway ... riding the wave of hands-on, over-your-head work for Jesus out on the world's front lines ... learning to handle politicians, the media, the agents, the editors, the interviews, and the fans and admirers.

Being married to Joni in those early days certainly kept the adrenaline pumping. They had circled the globe, served the desperately needy, reasoned with indifferent foreign officials, stood in front of eager, even wildly excited crowds, and racked up more adventures and improbable experiences in more exotic places together in just a few years than many couples would encounter in a lifetime.

But then they would come back home, unpack the suitcases, develop their pictures, iron out their digestion, get over their jet lag, restock the pantry, pay the household bills, and allow the adrenaline to quietly drain away. The vision of exotic landscapes and crowded marketplaces on narrow streets would fade. Ken would step back into his role as teacher and coach, and Joni would reengage with the machinery of a worldwide ministry that bore her name.

It was back to normal life.

So to speak.

In reality, living with quadriplegia was never "normal," and even the most compelling of international escapades began to fade after a while. For Ken, what *didn't* fade was the daily-nightly-daily-nightly drudgery of Joni's disability routines.

- *Help Joni get up ...*
- *Clean up breakfast dishes (don't women do this?) ...*
- *Pick up groceries (isn't this another female thing?) ...*
- *Help Joni sort through her things when she comes home from work ...*
- *Put away the dishes while Judy or one of the other women gets Joni ready for bed ...*
- *Turn Joni and tuck her in with pillows ...*
- *Get up in the night when she calls to turn her again ... and again ...*
- *Help Joni get up the next morning ...*

He remembered a story Chuck Swindoll had once told about his boyhood in the Gulf Coast region of Texas. A longtime family friend, a venerable old black man named Coats, would sometimes rub a leathery hand across young Swindoll's blond crew cut. "Little Charles," he would say with a sigh, "the thing about life is that it's so *daily*."

And so it was. The days of those nonstop routines became weeks, the weeks flowed into months, and the months rolled into years.

It was a thousand and one things, done over and over. And no one, unless they also had care responsibilities for a person with severe disabilities, seemed to really understand. Little irritating things that stacked up and weighed a person down. Getting urine on his fingers while emptying her leg bag. Washing her underwear. Picking up her medications. Hassling with insurance companies over coverage. Wading through a never-diminishing stack of medical forms and paperwork. It was like climbing a mountain where you took one step ahead and slid back two; instead of making progress, you felt like you were going backward. No matter how diligently you worked at it, you were never "done."

Sometimes he found himself asking, *How did I get here? Why is everything so hard? Why don't things ever get better?*

At the high school, people looked up to Ken. His colleagues respected him; the administration valued him; the kids loved the friendly, fair, approachable "Mr. Tada" — or "Coach," as his football players called him — and he felt like everything was under control. In Joni's world, he might as well have been the invisible man. No one seemed to pay much attention to him or ask his opinions. Or if they did, it was obligatory, or a kind of formality. Flight arrangements? Joni's speaking schedule? He always felt like things were decided by the time the questions reached him. He was always in her shadow. When they went anywhere together, he was her "Hawaiian" tour guide, just like on their honeymoon.

Somewhere along the way, the never-ending demands became abrasive, scraping away at the romance of their marriage, grinding down perilously their resolve to go on.

SATURDAY, SEPTEMBER 9, 1995

It was a Saturday afternoon, and Judy was helping Joni into the van after several hours of looking for sales at the mall.

"Joni, did you remember I have a church meeting tonight? It means I'll have to drop you off at home early."

As she secured Joni's wheelchair in the van, Judy looked at her face. "I thought so … You *didn't* remember, did you?"

"Well … no."

"Do you think it will be OK … with Ken?"

And that was the question, wasn't it? Joni wasn't at all sure it would be OK with Ken. This meant Ken would have to get her ready and put her to bed by himself that night. It meant he wouldn't get his "space" on the one day of the week when he really wanted it.

Bother!

Judy glanced at Joni in the rearview mirror before starting the van. Joni smiled a wan little smile and gave her friend a knowing look. It was one of those things they never talked about but both understood very well. Judy was well aware of the tension — even depression — that dropping off Joni early might cause Ken.

"Think you'll be OK with doing dinner?" Judy asked.

Joni felt her pulse quicken and a wave of anxiety tighten the muscles in her neck. She didn't want to ask Judy to stop by the market and pick up something — that might make her late for her meeting. But for the life of her, she had no idea what was in the refrigerator at home. What could she say?

"Sure," she said as she forced a smile, "it'll be fine."

She chose the word "it" rather than "Ken." She knew very well that her husband would not be fine, and a neutral reference to the situation, at least, wasn't a lie. Ken didn't like surprises … changes in plans … especially on a Saturday afternoon.

Saturday afternoons were semisacred. Ken needed the time to be alone, to unwind, to sort things out. Especially these days.

"We'd better call him, though," Joni added. "Let him know what's up."

It was a nice way of saying that a change in Saturday plans, especially dinner plans, would be greeted with reluctance. Ken wouldn't say that (there was a whole lot that Ken wouldn't *say*), but both Judy and Joni knew it was true.

Before Judy turned the ignition, she dialed the phone number and put it on speakerphone. It rang a few times, and then Ken, in a tired voice, answered. "Hullo?"

"Hon, Judy has to be at church tonight. I'm sorry I didn't mention this earlier..." Already Joni knew this was a burr under Ken's saddle. To have "not mentioned it earlier" only reinforced that she wasn't thinking ahead. From Ken's perspective it seemed like Joni never thought ahead when it concerned changes in the weekend routine; she had no problem if it was office stuff, but Ken's weekends?

That's right, she thought to herself, with a slight edge of bitterness. *They are KEN's weekends, not mine. They aren't even OUR weekends.*

Her throat was tight, but she tried to sound as normal as possible. "And can we do leftovers tonight?" She had no idea if there were leftovers in the fridge. And she knew that Ken knew it too.

Judy gunned the engine up the hill on Cairnloch Street, but slowed on the approach to Joni and Ken's house. Joni leaned down from her position in the back of the van to see if — yep, there he was. Ken was standing in the driveway, hands in the pockets of his down jacket and, even though there was a chill in the late-afternoon air, wearing flip-flops and shorts. And, yep, he looked irritated too. She could tell by the way he kept looking down at the driveway bricks, rolling his tongue against the inside of his jaw — his typical signal of impatience and irritation.

"Hi, Hon!" Joni called out from the back as the automatic side door opened. Without saying a word, Ken walked up to the van and waited for the automatic lift to lower. It didn't. *Drat!* Joni thought. *Of all times for this thing to give out on us!* Ken pursed his lips and grabbed the handle on the side of the lift to lower it manually. Just one more reminder of quadriplegia and how inconvenient it was. (Or how inconvenient *she* was?) Joni backed her chair down the ramp with Ken holding the wheelchair handles, but she moved a little too fast, nearly running over his toes.

"Watch it!" Ken groused, jumping out of the way. One more "quadriplegic thing" to further dampen the already depressing situation. As she turned her wheelchair, Joni sought out Ken's eyes, but he was still looking down.

"Are you guys OK?" Judy called from the driver's seat.

"We've got it." Ken tried to equal the strength in her voice. As Judy wound up the passenger window, Ken turned toward the front door with Joni still behind him. The van pulled away, and a hollowness filled Joni's chest. She followed Ken up the winding brick walk, past the blooming flowerbeds, then under the veranda and into the house — a lovely, classic, California ranch-style rambler with tan stucco and a red-tiled roof. It was her home, but it sure didn't feel like it. Instead, she felt a growing sense of dread over what looked to be another tense — and very long — evening.

They had cold leftovers for dinner that night. When it was time for bed, Ken mechanically washed Joni's face, flossed and brushed her teeth, and helped her into her nightclothes. Neither of them spoke.

How odd this is, Joni thought to herself. It seemed so strange to go through such an intimate routine without being personal, without any talking or feeling "connected." But things were looking up; she'd soon be by herself in bed. Ken would pull up her blanket, fluff the pillow, turn on the TV, leave the room, and go back to his fishing magazines. It was pretty much what he always did.

Only this time he didn't.

When it came time for him to walk out of the room, he paused by the dresser. After a long, quiet moment Joni asked, "Is there something you want to say?"

Ken folded his arms across his chest and leaned back against the dresser.

"This isn't right," he said quietly. She waited, unconsciously holding her breath. "I mean," he said, "about things being so tense between us. It's not right." With those few short words, Joni's chest felt lighter, and she could breathe easier.

This was so like Ken. So like the man she had fallen in love with back in the 1980s.

Yes, she knew he wrestled with depression, and that it went back to before they'd ever met. That was a comfort, in a strange sort of way. And yes, she was well aware that in recent years he was feeling increasingly trapped by her paralysis, which in turn pushed him into deeper depression.

But Joni knew his heart. Knew his integrity. Knew he would stick with his vows to be with her "for better or worse," even when "worse" seemed like a very steep hill to climb.

She offered an olive branch of sorts: "My disability puts a lot of pressure on you, doesn't it?"

He nodded, his arms still folded, his mouth working, not trusting himself to speak. There was another long silence. It was a delicate moment, and Joni knew better than to push the point.

"Well, I can understand," she said. "And, oh, Ken, if I were you, I would feel *exactly* the same way." Ken wiped his eyes and nodded again. She continued. "And I don't blame you one bit. I don't know what I would do if I were married to me. I just … don't know what I'd do about it."

Suddenly it felt as though someone had released the steam from a pressure cooker. The whole room felt lighter. For both of them. They both realized nothing "new" could be said about quadriplegia and marriage; it was what it was, and there was no bright lightbulb that suddenly flicked on. But just *saying* these words out loud, just voicing the truth without pointing fingers or casting blame, well … it was exactly what had been needed in the moment.

Finally, Ken spoke, saying typical Ken words.

"I think we should pray," he said softly.

And so they did.

This sentiment of "I understand" and "thank you for understanding" turned into a litany that would be repeated from time to time through those years. Not much was ever added to it, and more words never seemed to be needed. And it was enough.

Until the day came when they discovered there was something worse in the world than the relentless tedium of paralysis, something that would make the boredom of daily quadriplegia routines seem like the good old days.

It was paralysis shot through with hellish pain.

SATURDAY, FEBRUARY 1998

"So, how is Judy doing?"

Ken prodded the fire with a poker, coaxing a reluctant flame between two lengths of oak.

"She sounded terrible," Joni replied. "She would have come ... but thought she'd better keep her virus to herself."

"Good idea."

Ken poked at the logs again, sending a few desultory sparks up the chimney.

"You wanted to go to Burbank today, didn't you? To help with your dad."

He shrugged. "It's OK."

"I'm sorry you have to stay around here all day with me."

"No, it's all right. Mom wasn't really expecting me. Anyway, I have some papers to grade."

It wasn't the answer she had wanted to hear. She wished he would have said, "Of course I want to be with you today. There's nowhere else I would rather be." But that wasn't how things stood these days. Spending full weekends together just didn't happen much anymore. Fantasizing about what she wished he would say went precisely nowhere, like all the other empty fantasies she had entertained through the years. If wishes were horses, then beggars would ride. And Joni would walk. And Ken would have a normal wife.

She had been trying to give him extra space on the weekends. Stay out of his way a little. Lighten the load a bit. She had developed these skills in the early years of quadriplegia, trying hard to keep family and friends on board with her and not wear them out or drive them away. So, on many a Saturday afternoon, as well as on Sundays after church, she would take off with Judy somewhere … anywhere. She might go to her studio at the office to paint, or check out the mall. After church, she might have a long lunch with Judy or catch a movie with some girlfriends.

Back at home, Ken would be napping, reading a book, or cleaning his rods and reels. If she had to be home on the weekend, she tried to limit her intake of water so she wouldn't have to rouse him from a nap to empty her leg bag.

But now Judy was sick and here she was, at home with Ken all weekend.

"Together" used to sound fun. In moments like this, it didn't.

Neither of them spoke for a while.

"How's the pain?" he finally asked. "Can I get you anything? Pain pill?"

"Not at the moment, thanks. It's tolerable today. I think the massage sessions with Paulette might be helping some."

"Good. Maybe I'll have to try her sometime."

Silence descended again. The atmosphere in the room felt heavy. Joni looked out through the patio doors at an overcast February sky. She knew she had a radio devotional to craft, and then … there was that book deadline out there. But she didn't feel like crafting anything, let alone writing a book. Ken pulled a batch of student papers out of his briefcase, settled into his recliner, and began methodically reading and marking. *He's in his world*, she thought. *The world where he feels most comfortable. The world where things make sense.*

The fire had dwindled again to a few sullen flames, and began to smolder. Maybe that last batch of oak hadn't been properly seasoned. She remembered the dancing flames of a cherry wood fire back in the old Eareckson homestead in Maryland. Her sisters. Her dad and mom. The laughter. But that was long ago and far away. This fire wasn't dancing at all. It was about to go out, and Ken was so preoccupied that he probably wouldn't even notice.

He's depressed. Again. He doesn't want to be here. He doesn't want to be tied down today. But that's what I do ... I tie him down. I've tied him down for years. And it's so quiet. We don't even talk anymore. Here we are, with a Saturday together, just the two of us for a change. And we don't have anything to say. How sad.

The pain in her left hip was edging close to unbearable. She wanted to ask Ken for help, but these days, nothing *anyone* did seemed to help. Lift her hip a little. Loosen her corset. Pull up her corset. Tighten her corset. Joni glanced over at Ken, engrossed in his papers. A pang of regret gripped her. But she wouldn't let herself cry. That would mean he'd have to get up to help her blow her nose. *I'm wearing him out. I'm wearing everybody out. Ken. Judy. Francie. All the women who help me. This pain has become almost chronic. Daily. Never ending. It's gone on and on; no one can figure out what's causing it, and I don't know what to do. Is my life beginning to unravel? Have I reached a limit in what I can endure? Have my friends and coworkers ... and my husband ... reached a limit in what THEY can endure for my sake? How much longer can we go on like this?*

Her morning routines had become increasingly difficult. Now when her friends began her exercises, it involved at least an extra thirty minutes of stretching and pulling her muscles. She would say, "Oh, could you please pull on my back muscle? I mean, angle your hand toward the headboard and ... that's it. Now kind of rake up my back with your fingers. Gee ... I can't quite feel that. Can you dig in harder?" Yesterday it seemed to Joni that the two women had given each other quick little glances, as if to say, *Can you believe this?* Mornings used to be fun. They would all laugh and sing and say things like, "We get to go to work for *Jesus* today!"

But not so much anymore.

Not since the pain had swallowed up everything.

It wasn't just "nagging pain," the kind you could shove into the background or paper over with busyness. She remembered the feeling as a teen of hiking in Colorado and having a tiny sharp rock in one of her boots. It would have felt better, of course, to stop, take off the boot, shake out the pebble, and continue on her way. But that would be too much trouble and bother, and her sisters would say, "Are you *coming*, slowpoke? Let's go!" Besides, the hike was so exciting and the mountains were so magnificent that she didn't want to take the time. She would rather keep on keeping on with a little discomfort than have to stop the whole marvelous expedition, even for one minute.

She had tried the same technique when the pain burst into her life that year. *Hiking with a rock in her shoe.* She had tried to forge ahead, to limp along, to keep up her smile, and stay on her schedule. But she couldn't. This was no pebble in the boot; this was jagged, twisted, razor-edged agony, the stuff of nightmares, that sent her good intentions and her normal priorities into spinning chaos.

All the activities she used to enjoy had become incredibly more complicated. Not long ago, she had been sitting in her studio, recording her Joni and Friends weekly radio program, something she had done for decades. On this occasion, however, she found herself confronted with a troubling choice. She could have Judy cinch her corset tighter, enabling her to breathe properly in order to talk but unleashing sharper pain in the process. Or she could loosen the corset, dialing back her pain a little. But then it would be a struggle to get enough breath to record.

Eventually, she did both. She read a page or two, stopped to tighten the corset, then read some more, stopping again to loosen it. She had finished the session, but it all seemed so very slow and took way too long to accomplish. And the end result — well, it wasn't what it used to be. Everyone looked beat at the end of it.

If quadriplegia made marriage difficult, chronic pain made it almost untenable. Joni could easily understand why Ken had pulled back in their relationship, why he let others handle more of her care and worry about her pain management issues. He was maxed out! Of course he was. Physically and emotionally drained from waking up three or four times every night to help her. Tired of all the endless routines just to keep her going. It was too much, and he had stepped back a bit, delegating more and more of her care, for the sake of sheer survival. It wouldn't help anyone if he slipped back into depression.

Years later, in retrospect, they would describe "negotiated spaces" and "demilitarized zones" in their relationship: issues they wouldn't talk about, subjects they would never bring up, and emotional bruises they would keep hidden from one another.

Ken needed more breaks. Many more breaks from being with her, caring for her. He needed to be out on the ocean trolling for tuna, needed to grade his papers, needed to relax with a diet soda — his feet up and a really good TV program like "Top Ten Infantry Fighting Vehicles" on the Military Channel. He needed his quiet weekends. *Of course he did.* It was understandable, given the fact that life had become so very intense.

Even so ...

Joni couldn't help but feel she'd been abandoned. It was like that time when she was five years old, at the beach. Her parents had left her alone on a beach blanket and went back into the tent. Other adults were all around her, but she remembered thinking to herself that Mommy and Daddy shouldn't have done that. Shouldn't have left her alone under that wide summer sky on that long, lonely beach with the crying gulls circling overhead. Something about that wasn't right.

Ken wouldn't have described it as abandonment. From his perspective, it was more like "total frustration." In the last year, they had sought out so many doctors and explored so many avenues to try to determine the source of the pain. Joni, of course, could never identify a source or a location — it was just deep and inside, somewhere above her left hip and she just hurt, and hurt like she had never hurt before. And it kept getting worse! Rather than alleviating and giving either of them a little space, it kept eating away at more and more of their lives.

Ken hated to see his wife suffer, but he didn't know what to do, where to go, or where to turn. It was like a math problem in quantum physics for a first-year algebra student. What in the world was he supposed to do? It made him want to throw up his hands; it made him want to hide from the interminable reality of it, if only for a little while.

And now, Ken wasn't the only one dealing with depression.

The constant pain was eating away at Joni's otherwise happy countenance. She'd always been upbeat about her life in a wheelchair and had been able to lean into God's grace and find the silver lining in the clouds. But this pain had begun to blanket over her bright spirits. For the first time since those dark days in the hospital when she was first injured, she was depressed.

The day was etched in her mind — the day when, for the first time, the pain had really ambushed her, shaken her like a slipper in the needle-sharp teeth of a terrier. For someone who supposedly "had no feeling," the sheer intensity of it had been shocking. Frightening.

And yes, it had changed everything.

AUGUST 10, 1997

She remembered the very day when the pain began.

Ironically, the setting had been picture-perfect, and the company delightful. After all, it was Holland. And Joni, Ken, and Judy were in the home of their Dutch friend.

If it had all been a painting, she would have certainly painted herself at that table, with those people, savoring that moment. But there could be no pretending on that evening. Idyllic as it may have been, she knew she couldn't remain in that picture one more minute. It was either call for help, cry out in agony, or burst into tears.

Right at that moment, interrupting that relaxed, mellow conversation was a hateful thing to her. Finally she blurted it out. "I am so sorry, but I have to leave the table. I *must* lie down." Her voice had sounded much sharper than she intended, and it had the effect of a piece of china shattering on a tile floor. The dining room fell suddenly quiet. She could hear a clock ticking on a mantel somewhere, and the coffeemaker sighing in the kitchen. No one knew what to say. No one really understood. "Please," she anxiously whispered to Ken and Judy, "I *have* to lie down."

She had to take her mind somewhere else, somewhere away from that driving pain. She thought of the dining room and the scene outside that window, just before she wheeled out of the room. Even in the pain and panic of that moment, her artist's eye had taken it all in: A setting sun casting a soft pink haze over the Dutch countryside. The image remained in Joni's mind, like a half-developed photo, as Ken and Judy found a couch in a side room, laid her down, unbuckled her corset, and propped pillows under her back. Maybe she would come back and paint that scene someday. So lovely! An outline of windmills, venerable willow trees, and cows grazing in the distance. And swans, gliding down the crimson canal, with white herons delicately picking their way along the banks. Their hosts had set a beautiful table, with candles, heirloom china, and tulips — yellow and red — in glass vases.

She hoped the dinner conversation could go on without her, but whether it would or not, she had to get away ... or really create a scene. How could she even describe it to anyone without sounding melodramatic? *An ice pick between her shoulder blades.* She had held it at bay through dinner, willing it to go away, trying so hard to enter into the lighthearted conversation, wanting so very much to hold that beautiful picture just a little longer, hoping against hope that the agony would fade. But it hadn't, and somewhere between dinner and dessert, it had become unbearable.

Judy tried to make her feel as comfortable as possible, as the aroma of fresh coffee drifted from the kitchen. And *boterkoek*! They were having freshly baked Dutch butter cake with their coffee. She listened to the conversation in the next room, much more subdued now, along with the clink of cups on saucers.

Well.

It couldn't be helped.

This attack — this was a first. Not the first instance of the distressing pain, but the first time it had absolutely overtaken her, putting her on her back. Over the last few months, she had done her best to smile through it and to push ahead with her tasks and her schedule. But not anymore. Uncomfortable had morphed into *unmanageable*.

She heard laughter through the wall. Was her life, as she had come to enjoy it, slipping away from her? Was it all a beautiful picture she could no longer hold on to? *Would the pain swallow her up completely?*

Joni had certainly known discomfort before. No one was ever really "comfortable" with paralysis. Quadriplegia was an unnatural life to begin with, as the body sought to compensate for and cope with the innumerable domino effects of being physically immobilized. In that year, however, thirty years after the shallow-water dive that broke her neck, Joni found herself facing a new adversary, one seemingly as vicious and unrelenting as her disability.

Back from the Netherlands, Ken declared all-out war on this frightening new attack on his wife, consulting doctor after doctor. What was it? What had happened to her? Was it arthritis? A broken bone? Was it organ related? They did blood panels, bone scans, and MRIs, trying to track down the source. At one point, they became convinced it was Joni's gallbladder, which, if true, would have presented an easy solution. But her gallbladder had checked out just fine, and it was evident there wasn't going to be an easy solution. During the flurry of medical evaluations, their depression had lifted a little — lifted because they were *doing* something, or at least trying to do something. It had become almost a welcome distraction from the dull, daily routines of her disability.

But when no answers came, when no causes presented themselves, when the pain kept grinding on and on, both of them were crestfallen.

As the weeks and months slipped by, everyone around Joni

Raising funds for disability ministry at the Cal State track

We're engaged.

*Doors swing open,
and she's ready to wheel
down the aisle.*

*Presenting
Mr. and Mrs. Ken Tada!*

*Kyoko, Ken's mom . . .
Takeo, his dad*

*A warm wedding-day
moment with Ken's dad*

Our wedding day — a day of celebration and thanksgiving!

Champagne-custard cake — a favorite

Lindy and John, parents of the bride

Prayers for freedom go up as the Berlin Wall comes down.

Touring Red Square before Billy Graham's crusade

After Joni shared her testimony, thousands surged forward in response to Mr. Graham's invitation to receive Jesus (10,000 were standing outside the Lenin Stadium, unable to get in).

Speaking in a Russian church? Wear a babushka!

Judy Butler positions Joni at an interview for Billy Graham's Moscow crusade.

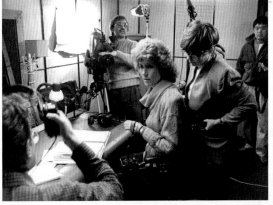

The first quadriplegic to ever crest the Great Wall of China? Why not?!

Joni and Dr. Zhang Xu — he came to Christ through the Joni book and translated it into Chinese so others could be drawn to Jesus.

Ken's high school honors their retiring teacher (they'd better; he was Student Body President back in 1964).

Giving Bibles in Cuba, along with wheelchairs

Fly from Cuba to Peru to do the same thing — this couple likes to travel.

At the White House for a stem-cell research press conference with President Bush

It's the dark back bedrooms where kids with disabilities are hidden — that's where Joni and Ken want to be.

Prayer is a huge part of Wheels for the World — yes, even in El Salvador.

An enduring ministry needs a permanent home —
the Joni and Friends International Disability Center.

Joni and Ken inspecting the pediatric wheelchairs for our wheelchair trips. The chairs are manufactured by the inmates at Taft Prison.

Anytime Ken sees a member of the U.S. military, he looks for ways to show his gratitude — this time, picking up the tab at McDonald's.

*Chemo behind her and
new hair coming in*

*Twelve months later,
a congratulations kiss —
"no evidence of disease"*

Airports are their second home.

*Getting into the spirit of Family Retreats
(the theme? "Come Fly with Me")*

*Enjoying down time
at a Joni and Friends
Family Retreat*

Kayaking — a Family Retreat first for a brave Joni and her oarsman

"Do-si-do" your partner at, where else? Family Retreat!

"Home is where you are" — even at Family Retreat.

*Ken and Jan on one
of their Wild Adventures*

Ken caught his tuna!

*Ken snags the jackpot
fish (Jan was bummed).*

Ken fly casts on a Montana lake — trout are hungry at sunset.

*Joni and Friends staff surprise
the happy couple with
a "30th Anniversary" party.*

*Don't smash it
in her face please!*

Ken Tada

Joni and Ken

realized she had entered some incomprehensible new phase of disability. She twitched and squirmed more in her chair, abruptly excused herself in the middle of meetings, and went suddenly pale in conversations, needing to retreat to her inner office where Judy and one of her coworkers could help her lie down or bring her a pain pill.

But nothing seemed to work anymore. Not muscle relaxers. Not Tylenol or Advil or Vicodin, or an even stronger drug than that.

Joni hated taking medicines. Born of her mother's and father's sturdy stock, a little German, a little Scotch-Irish, with some Swedish thrown in for good measure, she had shared her family's solid constitution. Through all her years, she had taken pride in the fact that she could push through any pain, relying on an aspirin or two at most.

But now she was desperate for help. Sometimes frantic. The pain would envelop her in a suffocating red cloud, leaving no avenue for retreat.

She had begun going to bed at eight o'clock rather than nine. And worst of all, she had to repeatedly wake up Ken in the middle of the night to turn her.

So far, her doctors had been stumped as to the cause of her razor-edged agony. The best they came up with was "myofascial exacerbation" or "pelvic obliquity" — vague terms that always fell short of a real diagnosis. One doctor had even recommended a psychiatrist. Say what? The pain was in her mind? She didn't much care for that thought at all. She wasn't ready to add "mental" to her list of afflictions.

As the months dragged on and the pain settled in like an unwelcome boarder, she began to lose hope that the situation would ever change.

Lord, please help me get through this ... or take me home!

She hadn't wanted to go there in her mind. But how could she not think about heaven without wanting release to go there? If she could just slip out of her body some moonlit night and make her way through the cool night air, up into the California sky to life, life on the other side of the stars.

Her prayers had been constant. And sometimes, if she was honest, they were more like accusations than heartfelt pleas to the Father. At night, when the hurt held sleep at bay, wild images would come to mind. Body and soul, she was like an old sailing ship in distress, caught in a storm, her sails in tatters, her fragile timbers battered, groaning and creaking under the awful pressure of wind and waves. Worst of all, her confidence in Christ Himself was being rattled. As long as she could remember, she had held to her belief in the sovereignty of God — His wise and total control over all things. Now, the very doctrine that had always illuminated her life seemed like a dark thing, foreboding and even scary. Did God really intend to leave her in this chamber of horrors for years to come, with no escape? Was that His "perfect will" for her? Endless pain on top of hopeless paralysis?

One night her fear had become suffocating. Ken had turned her on her side, situated her pillows, and then climbed into bed, trying to get some rest before his alarm rang at 5:30 a.m. for work. He had said nothing, not a word, moving mechanically, trying to stay half asleep so he could sleep again. Joni fell in and out of sleep until 2:00 a.m., when she was awakened by a searing pain. Was it in her neck? Wherever it had started, it migrated into her shoulder, *the shoulder she was lying on.* She twisted her head, seeking relief, but could only move in quarter inches, if that, to adjust her position.

She couldn't turn herself. She needed Ken. But how could she wake him up ... again? He wasn't getting adequate rest, and at that time, he still had a full slate of teaching and coaching responsibilities, parent-teacher meetings, and all the rest of it. But dear Lord, the pain! *Here I am*, she thought to herself, *a quadriplegic lying in a contorted, stiff position, and the only part of me that I can feel, well, it hurts like crazy!*

She wanted to pray, but the words wouldn't come. Instead, she simply whispered the name of her Lord, over and over.

Jesus, Jesus, Jesus. Take a deep breath. *Jesus, Jesus, Jesus.*

How could God allow this? How could she go on trusting in heaven among these splashes from hell? Sleeplessness kept her mind buzzing. *God, You are the One who is allowing this. You are sovereign! That means You have screened this and decided You would allow it to touch me, hurt me, tear me up like this. How can You permit this terrible pain, in addition to my quadriplegia?*

 ❧

Suffering was like fire. A little of it, in measured proportions, can bring strength to a life, pull a family together, draw a soul to Christ, accomplish good things. But let that fire break out of its bounds, and it can quickly become a destroyer.

She remembered the night, years ago, when she and Ken had gone camping in the High Sierras. On a cold, star-strewn night, she had been sitting in her wheelchair, savoring the warmth and ambiance of a campfire. Ken had gone to fill up a canteen, and she had remained by the fire pit, listening to the sound of the wind in the pine trees and staring into orange-red coals.

Suddenly, a gust of wind changed the whole picture. The flames vaulted higher, and Joni was enveloped in a choking cloud of smoke. Unable to wheel herself away or even to cry out, she could only sit and watch as the growing flames began to lick around her feet. Would she be seriously burned? What could she do?

At that instant, Ken had returned, dropped the canteen, and ran to push her wheelchair out of the path of smoke and fire. The campfire, her friend, had turned on her and might have destroyed her.

So it was with suffering. It had much potential for good — good she had already experienced in her life, her ministry, her marriage. But what if some dark night the campfire became an inferno? What then?

APRIL 10, 1999

As Joni suspected, Ken wasn't getting nearly enough sleep. It wasn't easy to be awakened out of a deep slumber in the wee hours of the morning, to turn Joni to a new position, and then to get back to sleep again, only to have it happen again and again. Sometimes sitting at his desk at school, he would find himself nodding off.

He did feel sorrow for her pain. They'd already been through so much together. He hated with all his heart to see her suffer, and he knew it was every bit as awful as she described it. But if a series of elite medical specialists couldn't find anything wrong, any source for the pain, what could *he* do? If God Himself had allowed this thing to go on and on, how could he help? Where could he put his oar in the water? Most men were wired to be problem solvers; if something needed fixing, they'd find a way to fix it, to take care of it. But this was something he couldn't fix, couldn't repair, couldn't stop, couldn't figure out. He was sympathetic, yes. And God knew how much he cared. But how much mental and emotional energy could a person pour into an insoluble problem? After a while, you just tried to live with it. It became part of life's landscape, like living in Siberia and stepping out the door every morning to feel the savage cold. Sooner or later your mind stopped saying, "Good grief, it's really cold!" You just pulled your hat down over your ears, wrapped your scarf tightly, and *lived* with it.

He had known from day one, back when they were fresh-faced kids in their thirties, that living with Joni's quadriplegia would be difficult. But not *this* difficult. It had, frankly, pushed him right to the edge. But how could he complain? What was his inconvenience compared to what Joni suffered?

The practical effect was that Ken and Joni began to find themselves on parallel tracks rather than traveling side by side on the same road. Joni realized one of the best treatments for pain was a good distraction, so she kept busy with ministry duties, writing books, and doing radio. Ken oriented himself more and more toward those areas of life where he had complete control: class preparation, grading papers, giving tests, and all that went with teaching. *And after all, Joni had Judy.* She had always had Judy. It made sense, didn't it? Judy had been with Joni for decades, having answered God's call on her life to help with the ministry. And Judy had a nursing background and was so much better at handling those particularly difficult challenges of Joni's paralysis. Ken wasn't even as "hands-on" as he had been in the earlier years of their marriage. It was just easier to leave it to Judy. Or Francie, Patti, or Carolyn — or whoever.

They could still move in and out of each other's worlds, but it wasn't happening as often, or as joyfully, as it used to. Joni had always had her schedule of events, ever since he had known her. When they returned from their honeymoon, she had moved right back into her Joni and Friends calendar of activities, commitments, appearances, interviews — and on and on it went. Ken could be part of that scene, sometimes, and enjoy it. But it really wasn't his universe. He had no say about it, no control over it. What he could affect were his lesson plans, his teaching, mentoring students, coaching sports, and correcting papers. And maybe getting away for a fishing trip now and then (with Joni's blessing).

Was it unreasonable for him to want a little time alone on weekends, getting away from all the stress and demands? On Sundays, he would go down to Burbank to help care for his ailing father, giving his mom a welcome break. Takeo Tada, who had wanted his son to be a hard-driving, type A businessman, could now be glad of the kind, gentle teacher his son had become. Toward the end, when his dad could barely even speak, Ken had sat in the backyard with him, singing hymns to his dad. And Takeo had finally responded, accepting Jesus as his Savior before he died.

Back home, however, both Ken and Joni realized their relationship had changed.

But then again, maybe it was inevitable. They had simply

"settled in" to a new way of coping with the multiplied stress and pressure of her chronic pain.

All her life, since her accident, Joni had learned to live around the problems she couldn't solve. What she couldn't change, she had to endure. She had also learned, early in their marriage, to temper those sky-high, unrealistic expectations of hers.

She remembered the time in the first weeks of their marriage when she had just finished reading a riveting little book on prayer and couldn't wait to tell Ken about it. Finally, they had the opportunity to talk as he helped her get ready for bed that evening, and she began to excitedly recount the new concepts and ideas that had throbbed in her thoughts all day long.

Naturally, she had expected him to be as excited as she was.

But he wasn't.

He hadn't been rude or yawned or ignored her, or anything like that. But then again, he wasn't sitting wide-eyed and awe-struck on the edge of the bed either. He had been … polite. He had smiled and nodded, saying a couple of "uh-huh's." But it was obvious he wasn't very interested.

Offended, Joni retreated into silence — the last, best refuge for someone who couldn't physically storm out of a room. Finally, Ken became aware of the change in atmosphere and asked what the matter was. After a bit of coaxing, she let it all spill out with a flood of tears.

Now she had his full attention! Gently dabbing the tears from her face, he gave her full eye contact.

"Oh, Ken," she had said. "I know it's no big deal. But I had been so excited all day to tell you about this book. I thought you'd be as excited as I was. When you didn't even pay attention to me — well, I felt so disappointed."

He had been gentle and understanding that night, but it had led to a discussion on expectations. She knew she had a problem with getting her hopes up about things. But so did he! Especially when she didn't ooh and aah over how many fish he'd snagged on one of his fishing trips. Nevertheless, he had said something that night that had stayed with her for years.

"Joni, if I met all your expectations, you wouldn't need God!"

Much as she hated to admit it that night, she knew he had made an important point — one she would think about for a long time. If husbands and wives were all they expected each other to be, neither would feel much inclination to depend on the Lord.

All of this thinking had led her to a firm conclusion: Christians should remember to place their ultimate hope in God Himself, whose love never varies, and who is always trustworthy, always kind, always faithful, and who never misses a single detail. And whatever life ends up being like on earth, our "threescore years and ten" down here is only the briefest of preliminaries to an eternity of love, worship, service, and unspeakable joy on the Other Side.

So was their marriage in some kind of survival mode? So be it. It *would* survive. Neither Joni nor Ken had any doubt about that. But in the face of great pressure, they had found their own individual comfort zones where they could "go on with life." They could continue to go along on those parallel tracks — tracks that remained geographically close and occasionally overlapped, but definitely went their own way.

They could endure it. They'd endured worse. Besides, it wasn't going to last forever.

Even so ... it got a little lonely sometimes.

And it hadn't always been that way ...

AUGUST 10, 1981

They were out on the lake in the High Sierras. She sat in an old beach chair Ken had wedged in the bow of the rowboat, closed her eyes, and listened to the soft sounds of the wilderness. The water lapping against the side of the old rowboat, the whisper of the wind across the blue water, the distant cry of a hawk.

Ken and Joni's boat had been chained by the bow to her dad and mom's boat, but now that her parents were occupied with their fishing, Ken had decoupled from them, allowing the boats to gently drift apart. Joni glanced at Ken sitting in the stern, concentrating on his fishing line. His thick black hair shone in the sunlight. His smile was ready, the corners of his eyes crinkled when he laughed, and as he had set up camp, anyone could see he was very strong. Judging from the way he had handled this improbable camping expedition so far — enduring the watchful, measuring eyes of her dad — he was patient too. His character seemed as clean clear through as the crystal lake on which they floated.

He knows the Lord, she thought. *And he loves my family. This is good. This is very good.*

They had been dating for a little more than a year and had become fast friends.

Letting his line drift, Ken slid the oars into the water and gently rowed toward the middle of the lake. Then, laying the oars across his knees, he let them drift again. The boat turned slowly in the water until Ken's head eclipsed the late-afternoon sun, making a golden glow around his face. Squinting, she couldn't make out his features, beyond his dark glasses and the white of his smile.

"Want to hear something I've been writing in my head?" she asked him.

"Sure," he said. "Let's hear it."

"OK, here goes. Stream of consciousness ..."

> *"Oh, the High Sierras, white-capped spires of age,*
> *Fragrant alpine meadows, paintbrush, pine all praise*
> *The God who made you and your redwood trees.*
> *Speak your mystery to me, High Sierras, just for me."*

"Beautiful," he said. Then, without missing a beat, "I love you, Joni."

She could hear her parents' voices across the water, and then her mother's laugh. Her dad had probably fouled up his fishing line in the reel again. Joni smiled at Ken, but she didn't answer.

He spoke again. "I think I've loved you ever since I saw you over a year ago, that time you spoke at that banquet. I tried to meet you and get close to you, but I couldn't get through all your admirers."

"Well, you know what?" she said. "I love you too."

They were quiet again, letting the wind take their boat where it wished, relishing the sweet wilderness silence, so far from the constant hum, buzz, and clatter of greater Los Angeles.

Ken spoke up. "It could work, you know."

She looked up at him, a question in her eyes.

"I've been watching Judy help you all these months. I know I could do the things she and others do for you. I could."

Yes, she thought. *You could. And you would. But do you have any idea of what you're getting into?*

"You're talking marriage?" she asked.

He nodded. "Our life together, Joni … It could be a real ministry for the Lord."

⁓

And so it had been.

Neither of them could or should forget the thousands, actually millions, of people in the United States and hundreds of forgotten, out-of-the way corners of the world who had been helped and encouraged in Jesus' name. By their ministry. Together.

God helping them both, they would have that ministry again. United as one.

Wasn't He the One who made all things new?

CHAPTER SEVEN

SAMURAI

*Fear not because you sometimes walk in darkness
and have no light. Remember that you cannot understand
the mind of the Lord, nor the meaning of His dealings.
But when the clouds compass you about, believe in God
as Daniel did; trust in the Lord Jesus at all times;
sing to Him in the dungeon, as Paul and Silas;
sing to Him even in the fire, as the three
Hebrew children did; be sure, be very sure,
he who believes shall never be ashamed.*

J. C. RYLE

In the first couple of decades following World War II, being
Japanese in the United States, even if you were American born
and raised, carried a stigma with it. As the only Asian boy in his
elementary school, Ken Tada knew what it was to be called "Jap"
by kids and even by some adults.

His parents had faced much stiffer trials than that.

Just weeks after the December 7, 1941, attack on Pearl Har-
bor, President Franklin Delano Roosevelt's administration issued
Executive Order 9066, compelling everyone of Japanese descent
living on the West Coast to leave homes and jobs and relocate
to internment camps scattered across the country. For Ken's
father, Takeo, that meant the Gila River Camp in Arizona; for
his mother, Kyoko, it meant Manzanar, a windy, dusty compound
at the base of Mount Whitney in Central California.

It was a distressing, shameful epoch in America's history. But instead of turning bitter against his adopted homeland, Takeo Tada vowed to "show them all" and become an American success story. And that's exactly what he did. In a postwar America, the Tadas returned to Southern California and rebuilt their home and their fortunes through sacrifice and hard work. Takeo went into the import-export business, bringing in crystal from Japan. Eventually, he linked up with an American businessman and began traveling to Japan to negotiate on behalf of his friend's electronics company, which meant he was often away from home when Ken was still a youngster.

Takeo Tada was a stern and exacting man, and he expected to see similar qualities of drive and determination in his American-born son, Ken. "Average" simply would not do; Takeo believed that a Japanese man had to work twice as hard as others to become a success in America. Once when Ken brought home a report card with Cs, his father sternly dressed him down to the point of tears. To the elder Mr. Tada, a C was as disgraceful as an F. Another time his dad walked in on Ken when he was coloring a map and announced, "You're using too sharp of a pencil." When Ken half-chuckled his disbelief, he got a resounding smack across the head.

In later years, Joni had once asked Ken, "Was there *ever* a time when you felt like your dad was proud of you?"

Ken had smiled ruefully and shook his head. "Well," he said, "when I was about thirteen years old, just after junior high school, my dad and I were going fishing, and we stopped at a Denny's restaurant in Bakersfield. When we were paying the bill, I stood there looking at a glass case filled with cigarettes and cigars. When my dad saw me admiring the cigars, he asked if I wanted one. I was stunned. Was he joking? Turns out he wasn't. When I nodded my head yes, he bought me a cigar. For me, it was a kind of passage. And it felt really good."

"How did you enjoy the cigar?"

"Well, not so much."

"So ..." she had replied, "he never really bestowed manhood on you, did he? You know ... his approval?"

Ken smiled, "Yeah, I guess you could say that."

The trouble was, Ken simply wasn't wired like his dad, and he could never find that same overpowering, fire-in-the-belly initiative that had propelled his father through the years. That led to multiple unhappy confrontations in the home, when he found himself being compared unfavorably to his older Japanese-American cousins who were already making their marks in the business world.

"Why can't you be like your cousin Randy? Why aren't you getting better grades? Why aren't you striving to get into a good college, like USC?"

Ken was genial and likable rather than driven and stern. At John Burroughs High School in Burbank, he was a favorite with his classmates, becoming student body president and playing linebacker for the JBHS Indians in the Foothill League. At football practice, Ken would occasionally glance up to see that his dad had stopped by on the way home from work. Takeo stood behind the chain-link fence that surrounded the practice field, hands in his pockets. He never waved or acknowledged Ken in any way. He just watched.

It gave Ken a small but significant glimmer of pride to see his dad standing there. But it was also a picture of their relationship in those days ... distant ... constrained ... separated by a fence neither of them could seem to scale.

When Ken turned down the football scholarship to the University of Hawaii, his father was disappointed. Turn down a scholarship to a major university? But the really important thing was that Ken study hard and get ahead. Business would be best, of course. Or maybe medicine or dentistry. Saying no to a scholarship, however, only seemed to affirm what Takeo Tada had already concluded about his son: no drive, no vision, no willingness to sacrifice, no passion for success.

In short, a disappointment.

ℰ

In the summer of 1967, young Joni Eareckson dove off a floating raft into the waters of Chesapeake Bay and broke her neck. In the grief and depression of subsequent days, she wanted to kill herself, even to the extent of tossing her head back and forth, trying to make the break worse and possibly, hopefully, end her own life. She felt strangled, as the psalmist described it in Psalm 116, by the cords of death. A living death.

In the very same summer, on the other side of the country, young Ken Tada had been invited to be a groomsman in a friend's wedding. The mother of the groom had given everyone tranquilizers, "since we're all so nervous," as she put it. The pill relaxed him, but when he drank a glass of champagne after the wedding, his head went fuzzy, and he couldn't seem to shake off the feeling.

That night, sitting in front of the TV at home, he still felt strange. Something wasn't quite right. He turned on some music and picked up a book that had been laying around ... *Rosemary's Baby*, a novel about the occult.

Suddenly and unaccountably, he started thinking about his gun collection.

He pictured one of his handguns. A .45. He visualized himself picking it up, pulling the slide back, and loading a bullet into the chamber, then going out to the front yard, putting the cold end of the barrel to his temple, and pulling the trigger. The thought repelled him and drew him at the same time. Restless, he began pacing the room. But he couldn't stop thinking about the gun. *What would it be like? It would be so simple. So easy. No problem at all. Maybe I should ...*

That night, before he went to bed, he thought about taking the precaution of pulling the firing pin out of all his guns, or maybe dumping all his ammunition out in the yard. It would be the "safe" thing to do. Or — would it? It would mean getting his guns out. Looking at them. Handling them. Feeling the loose bullets in the palm of his hand.

He didn't want anything to do with those guns. Not tonight! He finally turned in and fell asleep.

For the next two years, not a day went by that Ken Tada didn't think about suicide. It was never an overwhelming compulsion; it was more like an extra shadow that followed him everywhere he went. The thoughts played in his head like the proverbial broken record. *What's the purpose of life? What's the reason for going on? What could I hope to accomplish? Why not just end the charade? It would be so easy.* Maybe his dad had been right. He was a disappointment. Maybe he lacked the drive to make something of himself. Maybe he wouldn't be of any account in the world. Maybe he wouldn't achieve anything. The empty years seemed to stretch out before him.

Ken knew nothing of spiritual warfare at that time. Years later, he and Joni would reflect on the fact that the same spirit of suicide and destruction had visited both of them at the same time, in the same year, in the same month, on opposite ends of the country — Ken in his home and Joni in a hospital.

No, Satan was not omniscient, but … it was as if the evil one had picked up some hint in the heavenlies, some whispered suggestion of how God might use the two of them, together. It was as if he wanted to destroy both of them before they ever met and married, before they could form a team that would snatch thousands of people out of darkness, despair, and degradation.

But God had His plan for Ken, too, a plan that involved life rather than death.

Although dealing daily with depression, he kept his heart tender, and in an era of so-called "free love," he had stayed away from drugs and sleeping around. From his earliest memory, he had always had a sensitive conscience, an innate sense of moral obligation, and a deep desire to "do the right thing."

Ken majored in history at Valley State College, now California State University at Northridge. It didn't have the prestige of the University of Hawaii or USC, but it was close to home, and on familiar turf. It suited Ken just fine. He played football for a year, but didn't see that leading anywhere, and so he left the team.

On weekends, he ended up playing flag football with a group of friends, including Pete Lubisich, a legendary football star at John Burroughs High School and later at USC. Everyone in Burbank knew about Pete, and Ken had been a little bit in awe when Pete had befriended him and drawn him into a group of guys who played in a league.

Two of these new friends included two brothers, Ed and Nobie Hill, leaders in an organization called Young Life. Ken had met Eddie when he was Ken's linebacker coach back in high school. Nobie saw real quality in Ken Tada right from the start, recognizing him as a likable, sensitive, sweet-spirited young man. One weekend he invited Ken to be a supervisor of a group of teenagers at a Young Life weekend retreat at Valindale Farm, just south of the little Danish village of Solvang, California. It was a picturesque place with white barns nestled against the dramatic coastal hills separating the beautiful Santa Ynez Valley from the Pacific Ocean.

The weekend sounded fun, but it was rotten timing. Ken had a senior class midterm coming up the following week. Should he go?

He ended up saying yes, a decision that would change his life.

He had convinced himself he could take his books along and "study in the evenings." Not a chance! He never touched the books once. The owner of Valindale Farm had often rented out his barns and bunkhouses to Young Life and local church youth groups. There were cows and pigs ... and lots of mud. The centerpiece was a big barn with large wooden rafters, a straw-covered floor, and hay bales piled high. The place smelled great.

One evening Ken, Ed, and Nobie were in the barn, standing some distance from a large bunch of high school kids.

"OK, guys," Nobie playfully challenged the teens. "See if you can take us down."

The kids readily accepted the challenge, and in the following instant Ken found himself swarmed by a mob of pushing, shoving, fighting, laughing students intent on bringing him down. He put up a strong fight, but the next thing he knew he was at the bottom of a huge pile of high schoolers, laughing, yelling, and fighting for breath.

He loved it. And the teenagers felt instinctively drawn to his warm, approachable personality. The words *teacher* and *coach* began to gain prominence in his mind.

That night when the speaker, Randy Justa, explained to the young people what the weekend was all about, encouraging them to go off and consider the claims of Jesus Christ on their lives, Ken knew the message was for him. He opened his heart to God for the first time. It didn't happen overnight, but the thoughts of suicide and moods of depression didn't seem to have the same hold on him as before.

Ken felt like Someone Else was there too, fighting at his side.

༄

So who would have thought he would end up teaching at John Burroughs High, just blocks away from where he grew up?

As far as Ken was concerned, it was the perfect job. When the opportunity unexpectedly opened up in 1970, he stepped right into it. He'd had some good years at JBHS, and now he was going back to work with kids, coach football, and … something else. Something exciting. Along with his friend Eddie Hill, he would be helping to lead the Young Life outreach at Burroughs, giving kids an opportunity to pursue fun, wholesome activities and to hear about a God who loved them.

The depressive moods and thoughts about suicide mostly faded into the background as Ken kept a busy schedule of teaching, coaching, going to Young Life events, and playing in some all-out, go-for-broke racquetball matches on Saturdays. It was a mostly comfortable world. No, he didn't have a girlfriend. Not yet. But his dad had pushed so hard, trying to fix him up with Japanese women — flight attendants, daughters of Japanese executives, and on and on — that he had checked himself out of the dating scene for a while.

In the meantime, there was football, his social studies classes, parent meetings, pep assemblies, and the occasional disciplinary issues in one of his classes. Life was pretty good. A little lonely at times, perhaps, but on the whole, it was predictable, comfortable, and under control.

And then at church one Sunday he met Joni Eareckson … and nothing was what you would call "predictable," "comfortable," or "under control" from that time on.

❧

When he first pursued a relationship with Joni, he hadn't given a lot of thought to the idea that she was famous.

She was beautiful. She had an exciting life. She loved Jesus. She cared deeply about others. She seemed interested in him. And yes, she was in a wheelchair. What else did he need to know?

Looking back across twenty-plus years of marriage, however, he had to admit that Joni's celebrity status was one of the forces that had shaped their life together. Because of who she was, Ken had found himself in a supporting role through much of his adult life. It was Joni who had been the up-front public figure, the author, the artist, and the TV and radio personality — the one who had spent time with Billy Graham and President Bush and leaders all over the world.

How could he forget that time in Romania, when Joni's van had been surrounded by adoring fans on a street in Bucharest, trying to catch a glimpse of her. *Bucharest?* Even then it had amazed him. She truly had become an international celebrity.

It was what it was. She handled it all well, and that had been OK.

Or mostly OK.

At first, to be honest, he'd felt a bit like window dressing when they were out together. People always recognized her or crowded around her wherever they went, wanting their picture with her, wanting to touch her, wanting her autograph … and generally ignoring him completely. Like on their honeymoon in Hawaii, when several people had assumed he was her "native Hawaiian guide" showing her around the island.

A tour guide! Oh, well …

Not that she had encouraged any of that. No, quite the opposite. She had always been good about trying to introduce him, include him in the conversation, bring him forward. She was proud of him, and she bragged about him every chance she got — how he was revered by his students, how great he was at teaching history. She had even written a devotional once that made reference to his muscles! But he also knew who they *really* wanted to talk to. Of course they did. Who wouldn't want to talk to Joni?

So as the years went by, he had learned the art of stepping back. At least when he was in *her* world. In his world — in the classroom or on the football field — he was relaxed and confident.

He'd stepped back to push her wheelchair, when needed. Stepped back to let her shine in the spotlight. Stepped back to let her lead in conversations with senators, agents, book publishers, government officials, and health professionals. Stepped back to give her the prominence in speaking engagements, workshops, media interviews, whatever.

Had he been comfortable with that? Yes. Honestly, he had.

After all, it had always been Joni's name that was important, not his. Not that he cared much about his name. *Kenneth Takeshi Tada.* Takeshi, Ken's middle name, was the Japanese word for *samurai.* In Japan's ancient past, a samurai was a highly trained warrior who served his *daimyo,* or master, with absolute loyalty, even to the death. In fact, the word *samurai* literally meant "those who serve." They were an elite class of warriors, considered superior to common foot soldiers.

A warrior who served.

Growing up in America, Ken had been embarrassed by his middle name and tried to keep it a secret. His dad had wanted him to have more of a warrior personality — a hard-charging, aggressive drive to take on all comers and claw his way to the top.

Which was another good reason to hate his middle name.

But all this was about to change.

JUNE 2003

Early in the spring of 2003, Ken's friend Jan Janura had given him the John Eldredge book *Wild at Heart*. Many of the guys at church had been talking about it, but he hadn't been particularly motivated to read it. In those rare times when he found himself with recreational reading time, he loved to dive into a meaty historical narrative, particularly those that dealt with World War II. Because Jan had given him the book, however (and would no doubt ask him about it), he thought he should make at least a token effort to get into it. Almost surprising himself, he'd found it intriguing and read it from cover to cover. Eldredge was a rugged character — an outdoorsman and adventurer who really knew how to write.

The book had good stuff about spiritual warfare too. It was a reminder that a man's fight with the evil one never stopped, no matter what else might be going on in life. Staying prepared for combat was at least half the battle. And war was never comfortable or easy.

One phrase from the book seemed to lodge like a burr in his memory.

Eldredge had written that men long to have "an adventure to live, a battle to fight, and a beauty to rescue." Ken wasn't sure what that really meant — to him, anyway — but he couldn't quite let it go either. Could this be something God was speaking to him, right then, at that very crossroad in life? Maybe. He couldn't rule it out.

Ken hadn't been looking for, or felt that he needed, some new statement of "life purpose." At age fifty-five those things were supposed to have been settled years ago. Something Eldredge had said, though — about life as a man — had stuck with him. Maybe it was because he'd been planning on retiring from teaching and coaching that coming fall. The worldwide ministry of Joni and Friends had been steadily expanding, and it made sense to serve in that organization, making himself more available to travel with Joni.

Even so, strange, unsettling things can happen in a man's psyche when he contemplates decoupling from a job he has held for thirty-two years. And it was more than a job; it was a huge chunk of his identity. Teacher, counselor, mentor, coach. He loved his students, and they had loved him. What would it be like to let go of his career and just walk away? Would he feel lost? Adrift? Maybe a little lonely?

That summer, Jan had invited him on a weeklong fly-fishing trip. It would just be eight guys, hanging out in a rustic lodge on Trude Lake in the Caribou-Targhee National Forest near the border of Idaho and Wyoming. During the week they would fly-fish and spend some time going through Eldredge's *Wild at Heart* together.

Ken had never tackled that kind of fishing before. He felt more comfortable on a tuna boat. Fly-fishing? He didn't really want to go, and dithered about making a decision. There was plenty to do at the ministry and with assisting Joni. Anyway, most of his favorite fishing trips had been out on the wide, blue Pacific, and he felt ambivalent about learning to use a fly rod — and all that fancy casting. Saltwater fishing ... now that had an appeal. Hooking into a yellowtail, sea bass, or maybe an albacore tuna — that was fishing! And studying the Eldredge book some more? Well, that was fine. But hadn't he already read it? Wasn't he already getting great teaching at church? In the end, however, he packed his bags for Idaho. But mostly because Jan had really seemed to want him to come, and Joni had urged him to do it. She had assured him she had plenty of willing helpers for the week, and that she would be fine.

"Anyway," she had said, "I want you to go, Ken. God might have something for you there."

Well, how do you argue with that?

To Ken's surprise, Jan had invited John Eldredge himself to Trude Lake that week to walk the group of eight men through the pages of his book. Jan had certainly kept that development under his hat! Admittedly, it was just a little more dynamic to have the author himself talking about the concepts in his book, and about how they came to be put down on paper, than just bandying things about with a group of guys and a study guide. It wasn't every day you could read a book and then ask questions directly of the author.

At the close of one of his lunchtime sessions, Eldredge had encouraged each of the men to get alone for a few hours to see if God had anything to say to them. After that, they would get back together and talk about what they had heard.

A few hours? Ken wasn't entirely comfortable with that. What if he didn't hear anything? He liked the time alone, and he valued the opportunity to pray, but what was supposed to happen? What would John MacArthur think of this "listen for God's voice" thing? Anyway, what was he supposed to hear? A voice speaking out of the air, or maybe a burning bush appearing before him?

He didn't see any burning bushes that day or hear any voices from on high. But he'd had some success with the fly rod on that trip, and he was catching on to the *Wild at Heart* theme that he had an adventure to live, a battle to fight, and, yes, a beauty to rescue.

The adventure? Well, this was certainly a new chapter of life for him. Everything would change that fall, and his years of teaching and coaching football would soon be in the rearview mirror. He would have his own office at the ministry, and some new responsibilities to chew on.

And the battle to fight? Hmm. Those dark, shadowy fingers that had once pulled him backward into depression and thoughts of suicide seemed to be in the rearview mirror too. But it was best to stay vigilant. Someone had said — Eldredge, or maybe John MacArthur — that the armor described in Ephesians 6 covered everything *except the back*. In other words, it was never a good strategy to turn your back on an Adversary who wants to destroy you.

Ken had always had excellent teaching, ever since he came to Christ. He knew all about the concept and the reality of spiritual warfare. But John Eldredge seemed to make it come alive. Up to that point, it just hadn't dawned on him that every day he was actually in the middle of a battle, and had been for years now. It somehow hadn't occurred to him that a relentless Enemy was out to destroy, or at least cripple, Ken Tada, robbing him of his joy and his usefulness as a servant of Christ. He thought back to that long-ago night when he first wrestled with the idea of suicide, the night he imagined holding a gun to his head. He shuddered when he remembered the book he had been reading: *Rosemary's Baby. No wonder I was plagued by thoughts of death!* And now? At this crossroad season of his life, it was only reasonable to assume that the warfare would escalate. That was a new and sobering thought.

An adventure to live, a battle to fight ... and a beauty to rescue.

His beauty. Joni. And what a beauty she was. Inside and out.

But did she need rescuing?

MAY 2004

Ken was just a little taken aback by the question.

He'd been in the van with Dr. Zhang Xu, a quadriplegic guest from China who was touring with his mother, seeking to understand American ways of dealing with people with disabilities. Ken had offered to drive him to an appointment in Los Angeles, and he had just merged onto Interstate 5 when the question came.

"Do you have a Japanese name?"

"Japanese name?" Ken said. "Well, I guess it would be my middle name. *Takeshi.*"

"Ah," said his guest, "and what does it mean?"

"It means a knight. A *warrior.*"

In the moment Ken spoke those words, a memory came rushing back into his mind, a memory so vivid that it left him stunned. Glancing up quickly, his eyes met Dr. Zhang Xu's eyes in the rearview mirror. He had been watching the change of expression wash across Ken's face in that same mirror. Did this gracious Chinese man have any idea what his question had just triggered in Ken's soul?

Ken had just come from another Wild Adventure retreat in Montana where the men had discussed John Eldredge's strong assertion that God would give a man *his real name*. His earthly father would give him one name, and other people through the years might give him mocking, belittling, demeaning names. But God would give a man his true and authentic name, a name no one could ever take from him. In a mysterious passage in the book of Revelation, Jesus spoke about giving His people "a white stone with a new name written on it, known only to the one who receives it" (Revelation 2:17). Eldredge had urged his readers to seek out that name, the name that genuinely reflects who a man (or woman) was destined to be.

And what God was telling Ken at that very moment, driving a van on Interstate 5 under the smiling, watchful eyes of Dr. Zhang Xu, was that *He had already given Ken his real name.*

Takeshi. Warrior.

It was a name he had been born with but had never embraced … until now. His dad might have been disappointed in him or dismissive of him, and might have concluded that his son would never "measure up." But the heavenly Father knew Ken's true identity. Who he really was at the core of his manhood.

And now was the time to step into that identity. To own it.

To be the man God had called him to be from birth.

❦

Part of the challenge of living all those years with disability had been Joni's fragile health. Life expectancy statistics for people with her level of injury weren't what you'd call encouraging.

In her private prayer times during those days, Joni had prayed constantly and with great intensity that God would stave off any new injuries or illnesses. It wasn't so much that she feared additional suffering, though that prospect was daunting enough. What Joni dreaded most was the additional strain it would put on her relationship with Ken. He seemed maxed out as it was, dealing with her chronic pain issues in addition to all the daily demands of living with a quadriplegic. The pain patches Joni had been trying hadn't seemed to do much for the pain, but they had given her a nasty side effect: gnawing, clawing anxiety. New fears knifed into her thoughts; old fears took on a sharper, serrated edge.

And she very much feared an injury!

How would Ken handle it if he suddenly found himself juggling a whole new set of challenges on top of everything else? Would it send him into a tailspin? And what would happen in their marriage? Sometimes it seemed as though they were barely maintaining things as it was.

Lord, things are hard enough at home, Joni prayed. *Please keep me from breaking a bone. Please dispatch a few extra angels to protect me!*

It was a little ritual Joni carried out — a game to bolster her and her husband: "Can you believe it?" she'd say, "I've made it this far without breaking any bones. Well, except for that broken neck thing."

But sooner or later it was bound to happen.

And it did.

It was the perfect storm of untimely, inconvenient factors — small occurrences that, together, brewed the winds of gale-force danger.

Joni and Judy were scheduled to fly to Pennsylvania with Dr. Zhang Xu and his mother. Judy was one of the most competent, all-around-capable people Joni had ever met, but — one woman responsible for two quads and an elderly mother who spoke no English? It was a disaster looking for a place to happen.

Ken was to drive them to Los Angeles International Airport and see them off on the initial leg of a journey to Baltimore's BWI Airport. Joni wheeled into the back of the van, navigating past a somewhat alarming stack of suitcases. How in the world would they get all of that stuff checked in?

Ken — and Joni too — would have done well to heed an old Tada family maxim at that moment: *in a time of extra stress, don't do things differently.* It's a thought, Ken later reflected, that probably should have been in the Bible. Solomon may have touched on it when he wrote, "The plans of the diligent lead to profit as surely as haste leads to poverty" (Proverbs 21:5).

"Ken, can I please sit facing forward? You can tie me down safely and ..."

"Forget it!" Ken interrupted her, clearing some of the luggage out of her way. But he hadn't meant to sound quite that harsh. It was almost a bark, and he'd really been trying to soften his tone. *Not the best way to send her off on a trip*, he reminded himself. "I'm sorry, Joni," he said, "but it's just not safe."

"Yes, it is," she insisted. "It *is* safe. I'll be fine. Please? I'll just back my wheelchair up against the pile of luggage on the seat, and you can secure my tie-downs to my big wheels. I don't want to ride sideways. I want to be able to talk to Rainey." Rainey was a close friend who served on Joni's ministry team.

Ken sighed and looked down for a moment at the driveway bricks, shaking his head. He didn't like it. It didn't feel right. But what should he do? They had already had some verbal standoffs that week, and he knew he'd been insistent (well, stubborn) in arguing his point of view. But this time he wasn't being obstinate; he was just worried. He knew very well Joni didn't like sitting sideways in the van. It was hard to see things. She liked to look out the front window. She wanted to talk to Rainey.

"Oookaaay," he huffed, helping her back into the cramped space. Within a couple of minutes, he had secured both tie-downs to her back wheels, stretching them extra tight to make sure she was secure. With Judy, Dr. Zhang Xu, and his mother in another van, they set off, with Ken driving and their friend Rainey riding shotgun. It would be Rainey who would drive Judy's van back after saying good-byes at curbside.

The traffic was thick where the 101 freeway merges into the 405, supposedly one of the busiest intersections in America.

And that's where it happened.

It was one of several things L.A. drivers had to watch for almost every day on the freeways. You could, for instance, experience a motorcycle roaring at high speed between two clogged lanes of cars. And you could also be clipping along at sixty or seventy miles an hour with seemingly open road in front of you when a forest of brake lights would suddenly materialize right in front of you. Ken, who had negotiated those freeways since he was sixteen, had just hit the accelerator to merge into a fast-closing slot in the carpool lane. But in almost the same instant, the car ahead of them unaccountably slammed on its brakes.

"Hold on!" Ken yelled, jamming the brake pedal and leaving rubber on the freeway.

His quick reflexes had avoided a potentially nasty crash, but the sudden stop threw four heavy suitcases against the back of Joni's wheelchair, rotating the back tires and tipping the entire chair over on its side. In an instant, Joni was dangling, half her body on the floor, and half secured by the chest strap to the chair. She looked down. Her leg was at an odd angle, bent underneath her. She struggled to call out, but the strap was choking her.

"Ken, Joni's on the floor!" Rainey screamed as she scrambled to unlock her seat belt and climb over the passenger seat. "I can't stop here," Ken yelled. "I'm in the middle of traffic! Let me get over."

Within seconds, they were on the shoulder of the freeway. Ken leaped out and ripped open the side door. "Oh no!" he cried when he saw his wife lying twisted with her wheelchair nearly on top of her.

Ken and Rainey shoved aside luggage, lifted Joni as carefully as they could, and maneuvered her back into the wheelchair. As traffic roared by them, they waited to see if she had sweats, a pain signal that Joni's paralyzed body gave off in the absence of feeling.

Rainey looked up into Ken's eyes. "Should we head back home?"

"No!"

Joni's reply was insistent, and she had "that look" in her eyes. Ken knew why, and knew how hard it would be to argue with her. She was thinking of Dr. Zhang Xu, all the way from China, and his itinerary, so carefully planned and confirmed. She was also thinking of her speaking engagement that weekend at Lancaster Bible College's graduation. She didn't want to go home. She didn't want to retreat. She wanted to plow ahead, figuring "it would all work out somehow."

Ken, still badly shaken from seeing Joni lying like a rag doll on the van floor, wasn't so sure. Not at all.

"Joni, we should wait," he said. "We should really wait to see if you get sweats. Something might be broken." Rainey, pale and wide-eyed, nodded her head while wiping tears from Joni's cheeks. So they waited two, three, five minutes with nothing happening. No sweats. No clamminess. No sign of elevated heart rate or blood pressure. Ken would have liked to give it another ten minutes, but Joni knew Judy would be worried if they didn't show up at the departing flights curb. It would throw everything into confusion.

"Let's go, Ken," Joni said. "Please? I'm OK. Really."

So Ken secured everything again, with Joni facing in a safe direction, and merged back into traffic. Even when they were at curbside check-in at the airport, however, while unloading luggage, Ken kept an eye on Joni's forehead to check for "sweats."

"You OK?" he asked.

"So far, so good." Her answer was just a little too bright. Definitely forced. She was badly shaken, and he knew it.

Ken felt like giving a savage kick to one of the too-large suitcases he kept stacking on the curb. Some warrior he had been! So much for "rescuing a beauty"! He'd let himself get talked out of taking proper care of Joni, when he knew it was foolish. He felt sick to his stomach with stress and regret. It was his responsibility, and he had let her down ... again.

An hour later at the gate, just before Dr. Zhang Xu, his mother, Judy, and Joni were to board, Ken was still feeling Joni's forehead with the backside of his hand.

"Ken, I'm all right! Honest."

Part of Joni wished he would let it go, but mostly she felt touched, and warmed by how solicitous and protective he was acting toward her. Ken, who had never in his life been able to disguise what he was feeling, had deep concern written all over his face and seemed genuinely reluctant to let her take off without him. There was no "passing her off to Judy to be on his way." He was definitely hovering over her.

Joni's body, however, gave no indication that anything was badly hurt. Even so, at preboarding, he knelt down to look into her eyes.

"You can still back out of this," he said with urgency in his voice. "It's not too late."

Joni took a deep breath, shook her head no, kissed him goodbye, and powered her wheelchair down the Jetway.

As the plane barreled down the runway and lifted into the air, Joni could sense the cabin pressure changing.

And just that quickly, something else changed too.

Her forehead suddenly felt clammy. Really clammy. Judy, sitting next to Joni, with Dr. Zhang Xu and his mother seated further back in the plane, noticed immediately. She ran her hands over Joni's legs, squeezing here and there, "Does this cause sweats? ... Does this?" She lifted the left pant cuff; right above the ankle, Joni's leg was beginning to redden and swell. That was a break!

She looked up at Joni, worry in her eyes. And Joni was worried too. "What'll we do?" she asked. Both of them knew she was already at risk — a quadriplegic sitting still in a seat for the five-hour cross-country flight. But now, if her body had begun to respond to some serious injury … well, who knew what would happen?

"Can you help us please?" Joni stopped a flight attendant, briefly explaining the situation. Within minutes, the flight crew had her leg propped up and covered with bags of ice. "Thank God I'm in the bulkhead seat and there's room to do this!" she said to Judy.

To herself she thought, *I wish Ken was here. He was right; he was right, and I wish I had listened to him. He warned me, but I wouldn't listen. He really does love me. I need to listen to him. I need to quit fighting him …*

A flight attendant stopped in the aisle. "Don't worry," she said. "We've called ahead for an ambulance. They'll be waiting for you at the gate." By the time they arrived at the Baltimore airport, it was dark. After everyone deplaned, paramedics rushed on board and lifted Joni onto a gurney.

Judy was troubled. "I can't believe this," she said. "I won't even be able to go with you to the hospital. Someone has to take Dr. Zhang Xu and his mother to the hotel. They have no idea what to do."

"That's OK," Joni said, trying to ease her friend's anxiety. They quickly parted, Judy heading to baggage claim with the other two, and Joni down a side exit to the hospital. When the ambulance pulled up to the emergency entrance, Joni thought the place looked vaguely familiar.

"Where are we?" she asked the paramedic.

"Anne Arundel County General Hospital," he replied.

And Joni was dumbfounded. *I can't believe this! This is the hospital they brought me to after I broke my neck that day!*

Thirty-seven years suddenly melted away. She was back in Baltimore, back in the very same emergency room where they had rushed her in, slapped an oxygen mask on her, shouted orders, and shoved her onto an examination table. It was the same room where they brought her as a teenager, so afraid and bewildered.

But not now. She smiled, in spite of herself. All of those years of walking with Jesus had marked her — with peace. Even though she was without her husband or friends, an inexplicable sense of well-being settled over her. Dr. Zhang Xu and his mother would be well cared for, and if she couldn't speak at Lancaster Bible College — well, they would call on a substitute graduation speaker who would have precisely the message those students needed to hear. And that honorary doctorate they wanted to present her with? It was nice, but some other time would work just as well.

All had been anticipated, all was in His hand, and all was well. She could settle back in God's sovereignty like a comfortable blanket.

Even when X-rays confirmed that Joni had broken her leg, she felt calmed by an overwhelming sense of God's presence. It was as if He had brought her here. Alone. In a cubicle behind drawn hospital curtains.

Why, Lord? Why here? Was it a reminder of His faithfulness to her through the long years ... how He had met with her in this place way back then, and was still at her side today?

In the dim light of her little cubicle, she looked around and saw all the expected things: a bedside table, an IV stand, a blood pressure monitor. Outside, beyond the curtains, she could hear the all-too-familiar murmur of a hospital at night — rolling carts in the hall, the sleepy chirps and beeps of monitoring devices, the soft sounds of nurses' shoes on linoleum.

But there was more. So very much more. The presence of Jesus was here, more real and tangible than anything else. That was enough for her. Forever enough.

A nurse briskly parted the curtain and entered, holding a cell phone. "We reached your husband," she said. "Here, let me hold this up to your ear."

"Joni? Are you OK?!"

Ken's voice was urgent and anxious. "Listen, Joni, I'm coming right away ... I'll be on the earliest flight out of here I can get!"

"Oh, Ken, you really don't have to. I'll be OK. Honestly, they're taking good care of me." Joni tried to ease his concern, but she knew it was pointless.

"No, I'm coming. And Joni?" There was a pause. "... I am so very sorry. This is all my fault, and I am *so* sorry."

His fault? she thought. *I don't think so.*

His voice trembled — and was filled with tenderness. "I should never have let you go," he said. "I knew better. And I shouldn't have been sitting here in my easy chair reading David Baldacci when you really needed me."

Suddenly, Joni desperately missed him. It was a homesickness for her husband like she had never experienced before. *We belong together ... We shouldn't be apart.* Her voice weakened. "Then please ... yes ... please come. Oh, Ken, I really do want you here."

They hung up. Joni looked up and smiled at the nurse, who was preparing gauze and plaster to set her leg.

"My husband's coming for me," she said with a soft smile. It felt good to say those words, as though she were somebody's beauty to be rescued.

"That's good," the nurse replied. "Every husband should be with his wife at a time like this."

I know, Joni mused, *and it feels so wonderful that Ken really, really wants to be by my side. Quadriplegia, broken leg, whatever.*

It was 3:00 a.m. by the time Judy had gotten Dr. Zhang Xu and his mother settled into their hotel and drove out to see Joni. Walking into the hospital room, Judy was a little surprised to be greeted with a happy smile.

"Didn't you hate being here all alone? Weren't you afraid?" Judy asked when she reached Joni's bedside.

"There was a time when I was afraid in this place," Joni said. "It was about thirty-seven years ago. They brought me here — right here — from the beach where I had broken my neck. But no, not now. I wasn't afraid. God has brought me a long way since then."

The nurse, touching up her work on the cast, gave a wry smile.

"A long way indeed," she said. "I read your book when I was in nursing school."

On the way back to the hotel, Joni softly sang the hymn God had put on her heart. That night, she had been trying to think of a hymn about feet. Finally, as they casted her leg, it came to her.

Lord, lift me up and let me stand,
By faith, on Heaven's tableland,
A higher plane than I have found;
Lord, plant my feet on higher ground.[11]

It became her broken leg litany the next day as they drove to Pennsylvania, a constant melody reminding her of God's protection and provision through the trip. The following day, with her cast leg raised on her wheelchair foot pedal, she wheeled onto the platform of Lancaster Bible College. The graduation ceremony was about to begin, and in just moments, she would give her speech. But first, the audience rose to its feet to sing the graduation hymn.

Lord, lift me up and let me stand,
By faith, on Heaven's tableland,
A higher plane than I have found;
Lord, plant my feet on higher ground.

It was the same hymn. But why should that surprise her? Or why should it surprise her when the college president opened the ceremony with the reading of Hebrews 12:12 – 13: "Therefore, strengthen your feeble arms and weak knees. Make level paths for your feet, so that the lame may not be disabled, but rather healed."

Yes, he could have chosen those verses because of Joni's wheelchair. But she knew differently.

Ken squeezed Joni's shoulder. The meaning of both the hymn and the Bible verses was not lost on them. There was more that needed healing in their lives than a broken leg. But the same God who knit bones together could also mend deeper fractures than that.

Ken had an adventure to live, a battle to fight, and a beauty to rescue. And yes, she really did need rescuing.

"It's a new day," Ken whispered to his wife. "A new day. I promise."

CHAPTER EIGHT

STEPPING UP

As servants of God we commend ourselves in every way:
in great endurance; in troubles, hardships and distresses ...
in hard work, sleepless nights ...
in purity, understanding, patience and kindness;
in the Holy Spirit and in sincere love ...
2 CORINTHIANS 6:4 – 6

JUNE 2007

On another fly-fishing adventure at Trude Lake, Jan challenged Ken and another small group of men with the same thing John Eldredge had told them to do back in 2004: *Get away by yourself and see if God has something to say to you.*

Well, here we go again, Ken thought.

He followed a trail to the upper part of the reservoir by the dam and found a wide rock warmed by the summer sunshine. Sitting down, he looked up into the deep vault of the wilderness sky and said, "Well, Father, here I am again. Your son Ken Tada. Is there anything You want to say to me?"

And this time, to Ken's considerable surprise, there was.

It hadn't been an audible voice, but it was absolutely clear, piercing his thoughts like a sudden shaft of sunlight. And he had no doubt who was speaking.

"Joni is the most precious gift I have given to you. You take care of her."

OK ... Ken listened to see if there was more to the message, but apparently that was it. *Take care of Joni?* But ... hadn't he been doing that, for all these years? What exactly did the Lord mean? That he should do more? That he shouldn't delegate so much? This was around the time when Joni's chronic pain issues had reached new and urgent levels, a situation that was emotionally and physically draining for both of them. Was that what God had been talking to him about? Supporting Joni in her pain? He wasn't sure. He told himself it was something he would have done anyway.

Even so, it certainly seemed like the Lord was challenging him to step up, to take on some new level of responsibility concerning Joni. What did that mean?

When he came home, he told her about the experience. She wasn't sure what to make of it either, but just hearing him tell the story gave her a lift. Was this signaling some kind of change in their marriage? Something fresh in the wind? A hint of something to come? Or was it all just wishful thinking?

Time would tell, she decided.

MAY 2010

In the spring of 2010, on another Wild Adventure excursion, this time to Abaco in the Bahamas, Ken studied a new John Eldredge book with another group of men. During their discussion time, Ken told the guys about a personal decision he had made.

When he got back home, he intended to take one full day a week for a month to just "listen to God," and then to journal whatever he heard. And that's what he had done. At first, he found it very difficult to concentrate. He would be sitting out in the backyard, hearing cars on the street, planes buzzing overhead, and even rock music from his neighbor's stereo. Then, over time, those noises had strangely receded, and all he could remember hearing were the birds.

He had felt very close to God that month. Closer than he could ever remember.

It's not that he heard God speak every time, but the communication line was certainly open. The sense of closeness with his heavenly Father, however, was all he could have asked for. It wasn't like those old days in high school during football practice when he had recognized his dad at a distance watching him through the chain-link fence but making no effort to greet or acknowledge his son. Not so much as a lifted hand. No, this was a Father who came near, just as He promised in Scripture: "Come near to God and he will come near to you" (James 4:8).

Ken had set his heart to do that — to come as near to God as he could.

In June, Joni received her diagnosis of breast cancer. And when Ken went to his backyard sanctuary to hear from the Lord, he found the line to heaven still open. God spoke a message of deep comfort. Ken heard the same words again and again. *"Be not afraid."*

He was so grateful that the Lord had drawn him into that quiet place again and again over the past month. He didn't have to go looking for the Lord in this time of heartbreak; Ken knew right where He would be.

And He was.

Then the words came back to him: *"Joni is the most precious gift I have given to you. Take care of her."*

"I will take care of her, Lord," he told Him through tears. "I promise."

And he did.

JUNE 2010

For as long as he possibly could, Ken had wanted to keep one foot in the twilight zone of denial.

When he felt the lump on Joni's breast, he had thought to himself, *Maybe it's something else.*

On the drive to the radiology clinic in Thousand Oaks, he reasoned, *Maybe this isn't what it looks like.*

The next morning at the clinic, the technician on the mammogram had only said, "We will need an ultrasound." *An irregularity*, he thought. *Maybe nothing more.*

After the ultrasound technician said, "This looks suspicious. You need to make an appointment with an oncologist," he thought, *Maybe this is benign.*

They did a needle biopsy, and the oncologist said, "I think we'll have to operate." He said to himself, *No one has actually said it's cancer. Maybe it isn't cancer. They don't really know yet. Not for sure.*

Reality wasn't his friend in those days, and he didn't want to think about it. It was as if something had been knocking, knocking, knocking on his front door, but he was afraid to open it. If he answered the door, then he would know what it was, and he didn't want to know what it was. He could ignore the knocking, fill his mind with something else. He could tell himself that the knocking was only the wind or the house settling, or that they had a woodpecker up in the eaves. He could tell himself there had always been a knocking sound like that, and he could just ignore it, and maybe, eventually, it would go away.

For Joni, answering the door was no problem at all. In fact, she hurried to the door.

She had been in such dreadful, mind-numbing pain that she welcomed this intrusion into their lives. Any change was positive — even a negative one. Her first thought had been, *My prayers are answered. God is about to deliver me.* Who wanted to live another twenty-five or thirty years with the kind of pain she had been enduring? Life had become like walking in knee-deep mud. Taking one step forward, sinking up to her knees, pulling her leg out, taking another step forward, pulling her next leg out ... Slogging. That wasn't anything to look forward to. That wasn't life.

So maybe the cancer would take her quickly. How long did it take? Six months? A year? And then ... release! It would be like looking forward to a Caribbean cruise. Only heaven was a billion times better than anywhere on earth. Yes, there would be some suffering, but what was that compared to what she had already faced? Could it really get any worse? Hadn't she prayed and prayed for some change in her status? She had cried aloud to the Lord for help, like David had done in Psalm 40:1 – 2:

> I waited patiently for the LORD;
>> he turned to me and heard my cry.
> He lifted me out of the slimy pit,
>> out of the mud and mire;
> he set my feet on a rock
>> and gave me a firm place to stand.

In this case, "the mud and mire" was a life wracked with constant pain. And what firmer place to stand — *stand*, not sit in a wheelchair or lie in a bed — was there than heaven, in His presence?

Her depression over her pain completely lifted the day she found out she had cancer. It was going to work out all right after all. There is an end to this. Just one more brief battle, and then — freedom! It wasn't a death wish; it was a LIFE wish. Paul had said the same thing, hadn't he? He wrote to the Corinthians, "These earthly bodies make us groan and sigh ... We want to slip into our new bodies so that these dying bodies will, as it were, be swallowed up by everlasting life. This is what God has prepared for us" (2 Corinthians 5:4 – 5 LB).

Slip into our new bodies. What a happy picture! She could almost remember how it felt as a girl when she slipped into a cool, freshly laundered cotton T-shirt on a bright summer morning. How, then, would it feel to step out of her old, pain-wracked, useless body into a fresh, clean, new one? And then run barefoot out into some heavenly meadow in the morning light, the cool dew blessing her feet, the trade winds of glory caressing her hair.

Paul had also stated, "I desire to depart and be with Christ, which is better by far" (Philippians 1:23).

She could easily lose herself in such thoughts. Heaven thoughts. They had helped her endure a thousand nights of pain, when sleep seemed out of reach. She'd written a book on heaven.

She had dreamed about heaven for years and years. And now ... what if the departure date was actually on the calendar? What if her ticket was actually booked? An e-ticket. All she had to do was wheel up to the gate and get on board.

When she thought about it, there was really only one thing that kept her from hurrying as fast as she could to catch that departing flight.

Ken.

She wasn't just "Joni" anymore. She had been joined, body and soul, to another. He was her soul mate, her life partner, her friend, her other half. How could she leave him behind?

And how would he endure it? Her quadriplegia had worn him down; her fight with constant pain had almost pushed his head underwater. What would cancer do? And if God took her, how would he handle being alone?

A few weeks ago, she would have been very afraid that the cancer diagnosis and the prospect of a mastectomy would have pushed him over the edge, that it would have been a bridge too far. But — how strange it was! — that wasn't what happened at all.

Something different was going on with Ken. It was like being outside at a moment when the clouds shifted and the light changed. Everything was essentially the same, and yet — the scene took on a different hue. A subtle shift of colors. A sudden softening of shadows. Something was up with her husband!

She had noticed it at the first mammogram. He had been with her through so much over the years, but somehow — how could she put it into words? — he was really with her in that room. With her in a new way. Totally there. Totally tuned in. Totally by her side. Not just physically there, but THERE there. Rather than pushing away, he was pressing in, and more attentive than he had been in many years. Even on — no, especially on — the weekends.

And even at that strange time in that strange place, it had felt ... comforting. Something deep within her had warmed to that, and wanted it to go on.

And it did go on!

Ken Tada changed, right before her eyes. Yes, Ken was Ken was Ken. He had always been strong, loving, kind, and true — and you could almost make his qualities into a Boy Scout motto and add "thrifty, clean, and reverent." This was the man who would come home from a day of teaching at school, and if some girl in his class had a plunging neckline, he would tell Joni about it. He would say, "I *looked*, Joni. I'm so sorry I did. I feel badly about it." God bless a man who would tell her things like that, so open and true.

So he was the same, but somehow not the same. He was becoming a new Ken. Or maybe more like the old Ken, the once-upon-a-time Ken she had married thirty years ago. The Ken who had looked into her eyes out on that boat in the lake in the High Sierras and said, "I love you, Joni. This could work, you know!"

In one sense, the cancer really had pushed him over the edge. But the edge wasn't what she had thought or feared. Rather than falling into despair, Ken had fallen into Christ, into a complete, head-over-heels, no-holds-barred dependence on Jesus.

He had always been there for her, but now ... now he was stepping up.

$\backsim$

What had happened to Ken was no great mystery.

At some point during the week after the cancer diagnosis, a thought he had fended off and shielded himself from finally took hold in his conscious mind.

And he looked at it, eyeball-to-eyeball.

This could be a death sentence. I might lose her.

Back in 2003, his mother had been diagnosed with pancreatic cancer, and she had lived out her final six months in their home. The images came back to him — his mother in bed, the weakness, the suffering, death closing in, the final breath.

Not long after Joni's diagnosis, he remembered standing at the sink in the ministry's lunchroom, washing out his coffee cup, when the awful reality of it suddenly swept over him. Quite unexpectedly, he began to weep, tears coursing down his cheeks. Whoa! He hadn't seen that coming. It was like one of those rogue waves at the beach that knocks you off your feet when your back is turned.

He had never told Joni about the incident — men needed to be strong, right? — but one of Joni's friends passing by the kitchen had seen him there at the sink, one hand over his eyes, his shoulders heaving. "Ken is having a meltdown," she had whispered to Joni.

It wasn't surprising to her. Ken may have been very courageous, but he was also tender. It touched her heart to think he would keep up a strong, positive front while he was in her presence but would break down in moments when he thought he was alone and unobserved.

For Ken, the prospect of losing Joni to cancer had changed everything, making all the baggage relating to her disability seem minor. Quadriplegia? It was so minor it was hardly worth mentioning. Chronic pain? Oh, my, they could deal with *that*. The major thing now was saving her life. As John Eldredge had said, Ken had a battle to fight and a beauty to rescue. Drawing deeper on divine resources, Ken took his caregiving skills into overdrive. He was at Joni's side through her mammogram, biopsy, mastectomy, recovery, and chemotherapy. He was her constant companion for countless hospital visits and oncology appointments, and her counselor as they sought out second and third opinions. He was on the phone with doctors, haggling with insurance companies, and keeping a meticulous record of everything in his spiral notebook. He was *on* this!

The change was obvious to everyone, and especially to Joni. And cancer or no cancer, she thought it was one of the best things that had happened in their almost thirty years of marriage.

She had always, always felt loved. But now she felt treasured. Cherished. Even beautiful.

Ken remembered the words the Lord had spoken to him in Montana as he sat on the rock in the sunshine by a dam. *Joni is the most precious gift I have given you. Take care of her!* Now he realized what that had been all about. God had been preparing him, getting him ready, calling him into a deeper, stronger, closer walk with Himself. He had needed to be ready for what was coming.

Everything else in his life, all that he had been doing to fill his days and occupy his time, suddenly seemed insignificant. How good the Lord had been to prompt him to retire from teaching and coaching back in 2004. He could be with her full-time now. Her health, saving her life, was Job One.

Sitting in the backyard, in one of those quiet hours of listening to God he had been cultivating, he had an overwhelming sense that this was his true calling. This was what God wanted him to do, and everything else was secondary. He was supposed to step up and take care of Joni in a way beyond anything he'd done before. He needed to oversee her cancer journey and be her advocate and help. He needed to stand between her and the many demands on her life. Who else would? She needed him to be strong. More than that, he just wanted to be with her. At home. At the doctor's office. In the van. At work. In her travels. Every day seemed incredibly precious.

And he would be with her. From now on, he was going to be there, no matter what. Wherever this cancer journey took them, he would be there. She would never, never have to wonder about that again.

One night, as they were in bed, Ken said to her, "I have it all figured out, Joni. I want to live one day longer than you do. That's all. Just one day."

"But that wouldn't work, would it?" she said.

"Why not?"

"Because if you had a stroke or cancer or a heart attack and lived only one day longer than I did, you wouldn't be strong enough to take care of me. I need you to stay strong."

He knew she was right. He was in his midsixties now, but he needed to stay strong. Stay alive. Stay ready. He needed to take care of himself and keep working out so he would always, always be there for her. He needed to be strong enough to lift her, strong enough to carry her. That was God's plan for him, and how good it was to know God's plan! What had he just read in J. B. Phillips's translation of Romans 12:1 – 2? "Let God re-mould your minds from within, so that you may prove in practice that the plan of God for you is good, meets all his demands and moves towards the goal of true maturity."

Lord, he whispered, *Your plan for Joni and me is good. I receive it with all my heart.*

e⁓

For Judy Butler, the New Ken represented a jarring change.

She, too, had experienced a calling in life to come alongside Joni, and she had been with her years before Ken ever came on the scene. Judy first met Joni back in the late 1970s when Billy Graham made a movie about Joni's life. She was working for the Graham organization and had been asked to assist on the set during the filming of the *Joni* movie. After the film was completed, Joni asked her to help set up Joni and Friends, a ministry that would reach out to disabled people like her. Through thick and thin, Judy Butler had remained steady to God's calling on her life — which was to help Joni fulfill her vision to reach the world's disabled for Christ.

Who, then, was this new husband of hers who suddenly wanted to take over everything? He hadn't said a word about it to anyone; he was suddenly just there. Everywhere. Now it was the New Ken calling the shots about how the girls got Joni up in the morning, how the cleaning routines ought to go, and about Joni's work schedule.

Just that morning he had told Judy, "I don't want Joni traveling so much. I want her to be relaxing at home more, conserving her strength." And what's more, the New Ken wanted to be with Joni on the weekends and drive the van himself when she had to go into work.

This last development cheered Joni's heart beyond words. In their December commutes, she and Ken had sung every Christmas carol they knew. In fact, the daily trip to and from the office became one of the best times of the day. Joni now regarded their van as a little "traveling holy of holies." No dark demon of harassment or fear would ever dare trouble them on the freeways because they were filling up their rolling sanctuary with praise, prayer, and singing.

It also gave them private time together.

For much of their marriage, from their honeymoon on, alone time had been at a premium. The only time they had in privacy was at night, after Judy or some of Joni's other helpers had put her to bed and said good night. Early the next morning, a new crew would be at the house, ready to get Joni up and prepare her for the day.

That hadn't left much time for anything approaching a private conversation. And if one of them had spoken sharply or hurt the other's feelings, it might not get talked about before bedtime, if then. But now they were assured of forty minutes each morning and evening to iron out issues together and resolve whatever had been unresolved.

All of this change, however positive as it may have been for Joni and Ken, was just a bit much for Judy. Once, as she was attempting to adjust to these multiple new realities, she had turned on Ken in frustration, right in front of Joni.

"Ken," she said, "you've got all these ideas now about how things should be done, but don't you realize that for twenty-eight years *you just weren't there?*"

Joni shot a quick glance at Ken, expecting him to react and to shoot back, "I was too there!" But he didn't. Quietly and simply he said, "You're right, Judy. I wasn't there. But I'm going to be there now."

When Judy saw that he really meant it, that this was "the new normal," and that he was really in it for the long haul, she began to relax. After all those years of being on call 24-7, it was something of a relief. She found herself with more time to do things and go places than she could remember having for years. It would be a new and adventuresome era for her too.

With Ken stepping in and assuming responsibility for Joni's care, a number of new horizons seemed to open up. As Judy stepped back from what had been her primary role, Ken and Joni brought in a whole new group of willing, cheerful women who wanted to help with Joni's care. There were new faces and skilled hands to get her ready in the morning and put her in bed at night. It dawned on Joni that she had probably leaned too much on Judy for too many years. It had seemed so logical, because Judy had always known how and where to push, shove, pull, tighten, and massage to help Joni manage her pain. But others could learn those things too, and now there were "fresh troops" on board to keep up with all the routines and to ease the burden on Ken. One night when Joni, Ken, and Judy were looking over the 2012 proposed schedule, Joni asked him, "How many trips do you want to go on with me this year?"

"All of them," he said.

Joni and Judy looked at each other and smiled. This really was a new reality, and it made Joni's spirit soar.

She remembered the time, early in their marriage, when he had come home from a fishing trip, settled contentedly into his favorite chair, and sighed, "This is great. I've really looked forward to coming home!"

He would have been surprised, she was sure, if he could have known how much that one little comment had warmed her newlywed heart. She wanted their home to be a place of refreshment for him, a place where he liked to spend his time. And most of all, she wanted him to be happy and at home *with her.*

And now he was saying he wanted to travel with her *all the time.* That meant she would never "leave home," because home was wherever Ken was.

On Sundays after church, Joni's usual routine had been to switch over into Judy's van while Ken took off on his own. The two women would do a little shopping, pick up some food, and maybe call Ken from the deli counter to see if he wanted anything special for dinner. Later, Judy would take her home and put her in bed.

Not anymore.

Now, Ken was there with her. Every Saturday. Every Sunday. Cooking dinners together. And on Monday morning, they would drive together to the office, sometimes talking, sometimes praying out loud, and sometimes singing together, but always enjoying each other's company.

In previous days, Sunday afternoons were long for Joni, as she tried to find things to do away from home and stay out of Ken's domain. So she would go shopping, whether she needed anything or not, check out the sales, or just go somewhere with Judy and have coffee.

Now she was home on Sunday. Home with Ken. A home that had never been sweeter. They might dig in the front yard, prepare some new dish together, or relax on the back patio with a couple of books. On rainy days, Ken would get a fire going, and the two of them would just sit and look out at the rain.

Back in 2003, in that spiritual watershed year for Ken, he had committed to reading through the Bible every year with a friend, and they would meet once or twice a week to talk about what God had been showing them. Joni had been happy about that development, but thought to herself, *Gee, I wish I could do that with him. I wish we could read together and talk about the Lord and what He's doing in our lives.* But she didn't mention it to him, and she certainly didn't want to derail him from this new "wild at heart" adventure of growing strong in Christ.

But then Ken's friend left the country on an extended trip, and one day Ken said to Joni, "Would you like to do this Bible reading thing with me?"

Would she! It began on that morning and has continued ever since. Every day they read several chapters from the Bible and talked about what God was showing them, and it became the best hour of the day. Even in times of great pain and suffering, when their marriage was under such awful strain, they would take the time to open God's Word together. For Joni, it was like a flicker of hope, a foreshadowing that their relationship would eventually heal and that a new closeness would still be possible ... someday, somehow. And so it was.

She remembered the verse she had memorized as a child in her King James Bible: "So then faith cometh by hearing, and hearing by the word of God" (Romans 10:17). It was true: reading the Bible together every day, come hellish pain or high water, had kept the spark of faith alive in both of their hearts.

CHAPTER NINE

UNFATHOMABLE DEPTHS

Joy runs deeper than despair.
CORRIE TEN BOOM

SEPTEMBER 6, 2010

Halfway through her chemo regimen, Joni had a chance to speak to the ministry staff about her progress. In the middle of her talk, she pulled off her blonde wig, revealing a bald scalp. Several people gasped, and then the room became very silent.

"This is what cancer has done," she told them. "And it's humbling. You might say it has exposed me to myself in a new way. I can see my limitations more than I ever have before, which just reminds me of how deeply I depend on Jesus right now. When you think about it, that's not a bad place to be."

Even so, the battle for Joni's life became very intense at times.

Paralysis.

Crushing pain on top of paralysis.

Cancer on top of crushing pain.

Radical mastectomy on top of cancer.

Chemotherapy on top of mastectomy.

Pneumonia on top of chemotherapy.

And intense spiritual warfare with dark, malevolent spirits on top of it all.

Ken Tada thought back to earlier days of their marriage, when "all he had to worry about" was Joni's paralysis. It reminded him of what the Lord had said to Jeremiah after the prophet had been complaining about some issues of injustice in his country:

> "So, Jeremiah, if you're worn out in this footrace with men,
>   what makes you think you can race against horses?
> And if you can't keep your wits during times of calm,
>   what's going to happen when troubles break loose
>   like the Jordan in flood?"
>
> JEREMIAH 12:5 MSG

Good question! In other words, "If you can't handle a few skirmishes with the enemy today, how are you going to get through all-out war?"

And the summer of 2010 had certainly been all-out war.

Which inevitably made Ken think of his middle name, *Takeshi*, and its tie to the samurai of his ancestral homeland. Those fabled warriors of old had confronted and confounded their adversaries with light cavalry, creative battle formations, short-range archers, and their trademark swords, curved and razor sharp. Ken, too, was determined to use every weapon God placed in his hands. Patience. Kindness. Vigilance. Perseverance. Hope. Prayer. Faith. Love. Whatever it took.

A World War II history buff, Ken knew that in every war a time comes when you have to throw everything you have into battle, risking everything, holding nothing in reserve. Isn't that what General Eisenhower did on D-day? June 6, 1944, might have easily ended in disaster. He might have logically postponed the attack, as many were no doubt counseling him to do. After all, the high seas and the weather over Normandy looked terrible for an attempted amphibious landing.

Men would be lost in the landing craft before they ever got to the beaches. Husbands, brothers, and sons. But if Eisenhower didn't act, how many more would be lost in a war that could drag on for years?

Ike's decision to press ahead, to throw all his resources into the effort, changed everything. Changed the world. Before the troops had set sail, he addressed them, saying, "You are about to embark upon the Great Crusade, toward which we have striven these many months. The eyes of the world are upon you ... I have full confidence in your courage, devotion to duty, and skill in battle."[12]

Ken knew that this was "it." This was D-day. This was Normandy. This was *the* battle of their lives. God had chosen Joni for him, and him for Joni, and the moment had come to throw everything he had into this fight with cancer. It was time for Ken the warrior to step up as he had never stepped up before. Joni needed him, and believing with all his heart in the sovereignty of God, he knew the Lord had called him to this very moment, to "such a time as this" before he had been born. Eldredge's words had never been more true. He had an adventure to live, a battle to fight, and a beauty to rescue.

But it was so devastating to see Joni suffer. To watch her struggle to breathe. To see her face contorted with pain. Able-bodied people suffered pain too, but at least they could identify where the pain was coming from. Quadriplegics, however, with internal communication lines scrambled or shattered, couldn't always identify the source or even the direction of the pain. And when pain isn't coming from "somewhere," it's coming from *everywhere*. Instead of feeling a lance of pain in the shoulder, for instance, it's more like being immersed in pain. It's nowhere and it's everywhere.

$\backsim$

Right after Joni's second round of chemo, a new front in the battle opened up.

"I'm ordering a chest X-ray for you today," Dr. Ashouri said, removing his stethoscope from his ears, "I'm hearing something I don't like."

It sounded ominous. Dr. Ashouri had warned them that lung

infections were common during chemotherapy. Within the hour, Ken was helping a hospital technician position the X-ray machine in front of Joni's chest. Donning a lead apron, he stayed in the X-ray room to help hold up his wife's arms while they took the pictures.

"OK," the technician said, "we're done. We'll let your doctor know if the radiologist sees anything."

All the way home in the van, Joni kept singing. That was not uncommon, but this time she was singing loudly, a concerted effort to break up any mucous in her lungs. "I surrender all," she belted out as hard as she could. "I surrender all. All to Thee my precious Savior, I surrender all."

As Ken pulled into the driveway, his cell phone rang. It was Dr. Ashouri: "Joni has pneumonia. I want you to pick up a prescription right away."

This was exactly what Ken had been afraid of.

The first round of chemo had weakened Joni's body, making her susceptible to infections — and lung infections for a quadriplegic could be deadly. But Ken was not about to let this new enemy gain any ground. That night, as the pneumonia began to gurgle up in Joni's lungs, Ken stayed vigilant. The slightest cough from his wife had him out of bed and by her side, helping her blow her nose, helping her sit up so she could breathe, and sometimes pushing on her abs to help her cough or just get more air into her lungs.

But this pneumonia was proving to be a powerful enemy.

The second night, Ken and Joni came to a time that seemed to be the "worst of the worst" of what they had faced together through the years. It was an anguished, turbulent nightmare of a night, as Joni's pain, weakness, claustrophobia, and nasal and lung congestion launched simultaneous attacks on her body. At the same time, hell seemed to unleash a savage spiritual attack of mocking, hateful spirits that chanted, "Where is God? Where is God?"

Ken, anxious and exhausted, found himself fighting a battle

on two simultaneous fronts — physical and spiritual. At times, in his anguish for her, he found himself arguing with heaven, saying, *God, what are You thinking of? Joni's had forty years in that wheelchair, and then all of that pain for years on top of it. And now she has to go through cancer? Now she has to endure chemotherapy? Now pneumonia?*

It was a grim, dark path for both of them. Life for them had never been what you would call easy, but this seemed more like David's "valley of the shadow of death" than anything they had ever experienced. People make wedding vows and say, "For better, for worse, for richer, for poorer, in sickness and in health," but now Ken and Joni seemed to be on the edge of "until death do us part."

On the third near-sleepless night for them both, Joni woke her husband up for the fifth time — once again, she needed help blowing her nose. Lying in bed, gravity was her enemy and her lungs were filling up faster than she could expel the phlegm.

"Here's some Kleenex," Ken said as he propped her up in bed. "Blow hard. As hard as you can."

Blow hard? Could she do anything hard? All the coughing earlier in the night had drained every ounce of strength out of Joni's tired body. She took in as deep a breath as she could, then tried to blow her nose. She missed the Kleenex and smeared mucous over Ken's hand. She groaned and dropped her head against her husband's arm. The simple act of blowing her nose left her dizzy.

"Ken, I'm seeing spots," she mumbled. "I can't ... I can't breathe," her voice trailed off.

Immediately Ken forgot about his messy hand and the wet tissues littering the bed. He rallied his strength and quickly put his arms around Joni's abdomen. He squeezed as hard as he could, coaching her and whispering, "Breathe. C'mon, Jon Jon ... take a breath!"

She had once told him, "When I die, Ken, it will be from pneumonia. That's what gets all quadriplegics."

But not now! Not if he could help it!

Joni wheezed and then dropped her head again. *Was she throwing in the towel?*

"Don't give up now," Ken almost shouted. "Don't quit on me —you can do it. BREATHE!" He gave another hard push on her abdomen, *"Come on, Joni! BREATHE!"*

There was a sucking sound, and Joni was able to lift her head and draw in some air. "Keep pushing," she said weakly. There was a rasping sound in her chest, but a few minutes later, she was able to expel more phlegm. Inhaling and exhaling became more rhythmic, more regular. Ken sighed his relief and relaxed his grip from around her middle. Both began to breathe easier.

That ... that had been frightening. He'd almost lost her.

But it wasn't over. As Ken lowered his wife back onto the bed, they knew the regimen would be repeated later. Hopefully, they might be able to snatch some sleep before the next coughing session.

Ken climbed back in bed.

Just before Joni drifted off to sleep, she sensed that the approaching hours would be particularly intense. And she asked the Lord Jesus for something special. In the dark, in a whisper so as to not awaken Ken, she prayed, *Lord, I'm afraid it'll be worse next time. Would You show up in some special way? When I wake up an hour or two from now—and I know I will—please let me see You, feel You. I need You, Jesus! Let me know that You're there and that You're with me. You have said You will never fail me or forsake me. Please, Lord ... may I sense that tonight at some point?*

Later that same night, when she woke up again, pain seemed to fill the whole room. The atmosphere was thick with it, like a heavy fog off Chesapeake Bay, with dark spirits darting in and out of the mist, taunting, jeering, whispering nonsense. More frighteningly, she could feel her lungs filling up.

She called Ken, and he came to her, stepping into the dim illumination of the bedside lamp. It was the third time that night she needed him, but there he was once again, so patient, so kind, so ready to help, deep love and concern written across every line of his face. He turned her body to another position, pushed on her abdomen, helped her blow her nose. Spoke words of quiet encouragement. Stroked her hair. Chased away the demons with words of prayer as he worked.

Suddenly, Joni turned her head and looked up at him, eyes wide with wonder.

It took him by surprise. Was she hallucinating? What was she seeing?

"You're *Him*!" she said.

"I ... I don't understand, Joni."

"Ken ... you're Him! *You're Jesus!*"

Fresh tears began to flow, and he dabbed them from her face with a tissue. "I'm not kidding. I can feel His touch when you touch me. I can see Him in your smile. I can hear Him in the tone of your voice. Right now! I mean it," she said with a sob. "This is what I prayed for. You are Jesus!"

In some of her writings, Joni had called suffering "a splashover of hell." But there were also "splashovers" of heaven, and this had been one of them. Heaven was wherever Jesus was, and He had visited her that night. She had called out for Him, just as blind Bartimaeus, sitting by the side of the Jericho road, had cried out for Him in his darkness and despair. And Jesus had come. He came to her too — on that night, out of the fog, in the middle of that battle, stepping through her pain.

And His name was Ken Tada.

Within days, the pneumonia began to retreat, defeated by the prayers and tireless efforts of both Ken and his wife. Still, to be safe, Dr. Ashouri postponed Joni's third round of chemo for a week. Those precious seven days gave the Tadas time to regroup. Time to reflect on what was happening.

With Joni's forced seclusion in her home, they found they had more time to sit alone and get perspective on what they were learning. One afternoon, while sitting by the sliding glass door overlooking their backyard, Joni mused, "Honestly, Ken, maybe some people think splashovers of heaven would be standing on some beautiful mountainside with arms outspread — you know, a blue sky, fields of wildflowers, a soft breeze, and not a care in the world. Life is beautiful! But I think heaven's best splashovers come in the midst of hell's splashovers. Or maybe I should say, a splash of heaven is when you find Jesus in your hell."

"So that's what you saw in me that night," Ken said.

"And what's odd is, Jesus seemed so near and present that night, so intimate — in the middle of pain and fear and darkness, I could feel the touch of Christ."

At the very darkest and most terrible of times, Ken and Joni would experience something fresh, something fragrant. Like somebody opening a window in a stuffy room and feeling a gust of cool air, maybe catching a faraway scent of lilacs or of a mown field after a rain shower. It was the closeness of the Savior, sweeter and more precious than they had ever known before.

If there were any lessons to be learned from the years of pain and now cancer; if there were any insights to be gleaned, it was this: suffering had been — and would continue to be — the thing God would use in their lives to draw them closer to Jesus. To show them His power to sustain. And to shine most brightly through them. Brighter than ever before.

This was the marvel they would always remember, as the children of Israel would remember the night when they walked between dark walls of water with a mighty whirlwind behind them as a rear guard. It was the most frightening night of all, and it was the best night of all. Ten thousand chariots clattered in pursuit on their heels, but nothing could touch them that night, the night the Lord Himself fought for them.

They continued to stare out into the backyard, letting those thoughts settle softly into their hearts. Neither was quick to speak, until Ken added, "It's that sweetness of having Jesus there, of listening to what He has to say to us in the midst of suffering. It's like when Adam and Eve walked with God in the Garden of Eden, listening to what He had to say."

The Garden of Eden? Paradise? In the middle of such a

nightmare of cancer, struggle, suffering, and congested lungs? On previous summers, paradise for Ken was fly-fishing up in Idaho. The Garden of Eden was wading in the Madison River in Montana. Those fly-fishing trips were usually with ten or twelve guys, and it was always an amazing time, something he looked forward to. But this summer — this July and August — during chemotherapy, he knew Montana wouldn't be happening. It was his choice, though. His choice to be with Joni during this difficult time. He glanced at her, still looking out the window, and smiled.

"You know, Joni, how I'd normally be up in Montana this time of year? Well, when I first started going up there, I couldn't believe how beautiful it was, looking out across some of those Montana mountain ranges. It was like a little touch of heaven. But it's a funny thing. I thought I had to go to Montana or out in the wilderness to find that. But in these times since I've been setting aside time to seek the Lord, to listen for Him, just sitting here with you, looking out across our yard, at the flowers, at the hummingbirds? Well, I've found my touch of heaven here. Can you believe it? Heaven is in our own backyard. And heaven is looking into your eyes."

"Heaven was 2:00 a.m.," Joni added, "as you pushed on my stomach and helped me cough! Unbelievable."

&

In *Wild at Heart*, the book that had meant so much to Ken, John Eldredge had talked about spiritual battles, and about Christian men standing together against the enemy and being a band of brothers. "Don't even think about going into battle alone," the author said. "Don't even try to take the masculine journey without at least one man by your side. Yes, there are times a man must face the battle alone in the wee hours and fight with all he's got, but don't make that a lifestyle of isolation."

Ken was understanding more and more about spiritual warfare and the importance of not going into battle alone. But he wondered, *Who would I want beside me in a foxhole?*

A week later, when Ken took Joni for her third round of chemotherapy, things felt different. He didn't feel terrorized by the sights and smells in the chemo room. He watched his wife as the chemo nurses inserted the large needle into her chest port. *She's not even flinching*, he observed with pride. He watched Joni's face as the nurse hooked up the IV and adjusted the flow of poison into her body. His wife just smiled up at the nurse. She was astonishing.

Later that evening, after Ken helped Joni into bed, he found himself thinking about Montana and what he was missing. The guys were probably sitting around after dinner and reflecting on the day's fishing. Ken looked at his watch. It was late, but he decided to take a few minutes before bed to jot an e-mail to his good friend Chris Leech, who was one of the leaders of the fly-fishing trip.

"Chris ..." Ken typed, "you're my brother in Christ, an outfitter, the quintessential mountain man. You've literally gone face-to-face with grizzly bears in the wild. You hunt with a longbow and can survive for weeks in the wilderness. You're strong and tough, like a Navy Seal. And I've always said, 'Chris, if I ever go to war, I want you in my foxhole.' I say that because I know you are a warrior, that you are fearless, that you have skills with so many weapons, and that no matter what, I'd be able to count on you and you would always have my back.

"But over the last year, going through this cancer journey with Joni, I've changed my mind about who I would want in my foxhole. As I've watched Joni and how she has carried herself, I've been so inspired, so impressed. When it comes to cancer, we've gone to war against it, together. And just recently it dawned on me. Yeah, Chris Leech is tough. As tough as they come. But Joni is the *real* warrior. Her courage. The way she has modeled Christ through the worst of it, going through things that even super-strong able-bodied men couldn't handle.

"So I'm sorry to tell you, buddy, but you are now second in my book. If I'm in a war, *I want Joni in my foxhole*. I want Joni fighting beside me. I want Joni watching my back. You may go one-on-one with grizzlies, but I've never seen anyone with courage like Joni. *She* is the quintessential warrior. I'm so very, very proud of her."

Ken took a moment to reread his e-mail to his friend Chris before he clicked the SEND button. Nope, he wouldn't change a word. His fishing buddies up in Montana were probably heading for their bunks right about now, pausing to step outside, stretch their arms, and look up at the wild, windy, star-splattered night. Maybe there were breezes whistling through the pines. The Madison River, just down the hill from the ranch, was no doubt hiding its fat fish, all of them resting for the night and dreaming of the next hatch of morning mayflies.

Did Ken wish he were there? He leaned back in his computer chair for a long moment, hands behind his head. Then he glanced at the door to their bedroom. No, he was right where God wanted him to be. And it felt *so good*.

The next morning Ken read his e-mail to Joni.

"Do you know what that means for a wife to hear that?" Joni said. "How many wives get to hear their husbands say that — 'I'm *proud* of you'!"?

Weeks later, somewhere between the third and fourth rounds of chemo, Joni and Ken felt a cosmic shift — yes, in their relationship, for they were so much stronger together, but also in their relationship with Christ. This cancer was turning out to be a severe mercy. A bruising of a blessing, and a blessing out of brokenness. A strange friend, but still, a friend. An unwelcomed guest, but still, a guest. God was using this cancer to open new vistas in His Word, as well as new opportunities to witness to others. A great many others.

While Joni was still convalescing at home in late August 2010, Dr. James Dobson, a good friend of the Tadas, did an interview with Ken and Joni. It would be the first time either of them had spoken in public about their cancer journey.

Dr. Dobson, with a little catch in his voice, said, "Joni, I know you've written a lot in your blogs about the whole concept of walking with the Holy Spirit. Galatians 5:25 reads, 'Keep in step with the Spirit.' You and Ken have been all over the world and seen many places, but walking in the Spirit isn't always about grand schemes or the big mountaintop moments, is it? It's in those very small steps we take with Him too."

"Yes," she affirmed. "And this whole season of cancer, chemo, and recovery has caused me to live life just like that. At this time in my life — fighting cancer — small steps are all I can do. I can't do travel or go out with our field teams or participate in our Family Retreats or take Wheels for the World trips. I'm at home every day, and right now, the Holy Spirit wants me to take life in very, very, very small steps.

"In the morning I will sometimes say, 'Lord Jesus, what would please You today?' And I hear Him reply, 'Seeing you eat forty-five grams of protein before lunch.' And after lunch I will say, 'Jesus, what would please You this afternoon?' And I will hear Him reply, 'OK, Joni, back away from your computer and enjoy the hummingbirds at your feeder. And this evening, how about giving the Food Network a rest and spending some time in the Word and meditating, praying, and singing some hymns to Me.'

"That's living life in very small steps and keeping in step with the Spirit. Cancer has a way of making me do that, and that's not bad."

"A lot of people at the altar getting married," Dobson said, "are thinking about the 'better, richer, in health' part of the vows, and they're not thinking about the 'worse, poorer, in sickness' parts. What has it meant to your relationship to go through the struggle of these last few months?"

"We have fallen in love with each other," Ken said. "I don't know how else to say it. We loved each other before, but I don't think we really had a clue twenty-eight years ago as we stood at the altar before John MacArthur at Grace Community Church. In this past year, we have fallen in love with each other in a new way."

"Mmm," said Dobson.

"Joni and I have talked about it, and I don't think a lot of couples get a chance at a love like this, at closeness like this. It's like all this has been a *gift* God has given us."

Joni agreed. "It's like a wedding gift all over again. I would have never thought this journey through cancer would have given us so much. At home we have a wooden plaque over our kitchen sink with the words of Isaiah 43:2 carved into the wood. It reads, 'When you pass through the waters, I will be with you; and when you pass through the rivers, they will not sweep over you. When you walk through the fire, you will not be burned.'

"The fact is, if God brings you *to* it, He will bring you *through* it. He will. And He has. And when we come out on the other side of this, wherever that other side is, our love and commitment and joy as a husband and wife have become stronger than we could have imagined. And my respect for my husband has just gone up notch after notch — just to see the way he has honored those wedding vows to me."

"This interview is amazing to me," Dr. Dobson said. "Here you are, talking about a time in your life that's been filled with such great struggles — trials you wouldn't wish on anyone. And yet you're describing it like a storybook love and romance. This really is a love story. It's not just a story of a man and a woman who have gone through unbelievable trials and struggles together; it's a story of your love and commitment and dedication to one another through it all."

"It is a love story about Ken and me," Joni replied, "but it's also a love story about Jesus. It's about getting closer to Christ, and experiencing Him in a way beyond anything we had experienced before. He pushed us out of the shallows in our marriage to unfathomable depths — and it was frightening. But now we know His arms have been underneath us, holding us up all the way along."

"That's right," Ken said. "The more we have been forced to depend on Christ in our weakness, the stronger our marriage has become."

"So what about the future?" Dobson asked. "What are you thinking as you look ahead?"

"We're not in control of events," Ken replied. "As much as we'd like to see into the future, we have to live day by day, like everyone else. And during that waiting period, we have to call on the Lord to be our sustaining force."

"I love reading the Puritans," Joni added. "How they're always talking about death, and the fact that really your whole life is about preparing to die. We have a PET scan coming up where they'll be looking to see if my cancer has spread. So life may be very different next year. But that's OK, because God will give us the grace. As Ken often says, 'Not one of us ever gets out of this life alive.'"

"I don't have the opportunity to be with you in person very often," Dr. Dobson said, "and even now we're just talking on the phone. But I can see you in my mind's eye, Joni, sitting in a wheelchair during this chemo. I can see you, bald and suffering the ravages of the chemo, and — knowing you, Joni — still singing a hymn."

Joni smiled. "And you would be right. That's just what I do. I sing because I have to sing, no matter what's going on in my life. Lately, I've been singing this Fanny Crosby hymn ..." And Joni began to sing into the speakerphone — and in radios across the United States and Canada:

All the way my Savior leads me —
Cheers each winding path I tread,
Gives me grace for every trial,
Feeds me with the living Bread.
Though my weary steps may falter
And my soul athirst may be,
Gushing from the Rock before me,
Lo! a spring of joy I see;
Gushing from the Rock before me,
Lo! a spring of joy I see.[13]

"Every morning I get to drink from that spring flowing from the Rock. And it really *is* a spring of joy. And every morning to pray, 'Lord, fill me up; help me this day,' is a privilege. And anyhow ... the bottom line of life is heaven. When I step over to the other side, I just want to hear Him say, 'Well done, Joni. Well done, good and faithful servant. I gave you a big challenge in your life, and you grabbed it, and you remained faithful to Me.' I can't wait to hear those words!"

"And Ken will hear those same words," Dr. Dobson added. "Only with this difference. Joni, you didn't have any choice about the challenge God tossed to you as a seventeen-year-old girl. But Ken did! He willingly chose this path, willingly chose the hardship and suffering it would involve. No, he didn't know everything, and the enormity of his decision probably hadn't dawned on him yet. But he willingly chose you and married you. Ken, you drew her into your embrace, and you have taken care of her all these years."

"I think you give me too much credit," Ken replied. "God gave me the privilege of having a wife like Joni."

"And I agree with Ken," Joni added. "I think Dr. Dobson is giving us both too much credit. It isn't about us and what we have faced in life; it's about Jesus Christ. I don't think we could daily embrace our cross without first embracing the cross of Jesus."

❧

Later on, after the interview was over and he had put Joni to bed, Ken sat in his chair by a crackling fire in the stillness of their living room, thinking about the interview, pondering Joni's words to him on that "worst of all nights."

"Ken ... you're Him! You're Jesus!"

It wasn't every day that someone mistook you for Jesus. It wasn't every day you got to *be* Jesus to someone. It was humbling. In one sense, if you really thought about it, it was the ultimate achievement of his life. What could he have ever done in life that would be more significant than that? His dad had wanted him to be a businessman. Suppose he'd gone that way. Suppose he'd become a billionaire like Donald Trump, with a big skyscraper in Manhattan named after him. *Tada Tower.* He laughed at the thought. Or maybe if he'd become a famous teacher, and they made a movie about him, like *Goodbye, Mr. Chips.* Would any of those things be more amazing, more eternally valuable, than having someone look at you in their pain in the night and *see Jesus*?

Through the years, he and Joni — together, as a team — had experienced the privilege of being the hands and feet and voice of Jesus to thousands of suffering people around the world … in India, Romania, China, Ghana, Cuba, Poland. They'd had the opportunity to bring hope and Christ's love to wounded veterans coming home from the wars in Iraq and Afghanistan. They'd had the chance to laugh and smile and cheer on kids and teens with disabilities at their family camps across the country.

Dr. Dobson and everyone else always wanted to talk to Ken about how *hard* it had been. How difficult to be married to a paralyzed woman and go through all of that suffering and all of those trials together. And yeah, it had been hard at times. Incredibly hard. And he hadn't always been cheerful or optimistic about it. His steps had faltered at times. He had wrestled with weariness, depression, and questions of self-image.

But he had stayed the course. And that thought filled him with gratitude.

Now, when she needed him more than ever, he was there — and he *would* be there, no matter what. He would pour his life into her, as she had poured her life, without reservation, into him. He would stand by her side, and they would fight the cancer with every ounce of strength that Jesus gave him.

After all, there was that middle name thing of his.
Takeshi.
Warrior.
His parents had named him better than they knew.

CHAPTER TEN

REFLECTING
ON THE JOURNEY

But I trust in you, Lord;
I say, "You are my God."
My times are in your hands.

PSALM 31:14 – 15

JANUARY 2011

It was a late-winter Sunday afternoon, and it was raining.

Ken built a fire and lit a couple of candles, and they sat together by the sliding glass door watching the rain. They both liked keeping the house cool, with the fireplace as their only heat source. Joni had her coziest sweater on, as well as a pair of corduroys, and Ken had his usual at-home uniform of cotton gym shorts and a fleecy Polartec sweatshirt. Off to their right, where the eaves of the house and the patio latticework came together, it formed a waterspout, sending a cascade onto the brick patio. It made for a satisfying splashing sound, like an impromptu fountain. In the distance, the Santa Susana Mountains seemed moody and misty, hiding and then reappearing as heavy clouds poured in from the west.

Glancing at her husband, she thought to herself, *He is such a good man. He was always a good man. He always did his duty, helping me like a good Boy Scout, but now it's more than a duty —it's a delight. He likes me! He doesn't just love me; he likes me and wants to be with me.* Such thoughts still felt a little new, like a fresh-from-the-store sweater that you know you're going to love and feel comfortable in for a long, long time.

As the fire popped and raindrops pattered on the windows, the two of them began reminiscing on their years together.

It was the sort of thing that probably would have never happened apart from the cancer surgery and the long hours of just being quiet together, in the shelter of a familiar and well-loved place.

Another blessing of cancer.

"Do you remember ..."

"How about that time when ..."

"I'll never forget when we ..."

It was like a slide show without the slides. Memories — some sharp and vivid, others with blurred corners and softened edges — kept the conversation and the laughter alive all afternoon.

And then it was time for takeout Chinese, moo goo gai pan, and maybe an episode of *Downton Abbey* on TV.

Joni loved Sundays.

FEBRUARY 1982

"I know who did it," Joni whispered in Judy's ear.

"Bet you don't."

"Yep. Yep, I do. It was that guy's mistress." Her voice had grown louder.

"Not a chance!" Judy had forgotten to whisper at all. "She was nowhere near when the murder took place."

"Shhh!" Ken had leaned forward, putting his finger to his lips.

Joni glanced at him. "Sorry!" she said in a hoarse whisper. She turned back to Judy. "We've got to keep it down a little. Anyway, I think the mistress knew all along about that ..."

The Agatha Christie movie concluded, and Joni and Judy broke into excited conversation and laughter as the credits rolled. Ken was silent, gathering up his sweatshirt and popcorn box and stepping over Joni's legs to retrieve the wheelchair at the front of the theater.

"Excuse me," he said, suddenly sounding stiff and formal.

"Uh-oh." Joni glanced at Judy. "Something's wrong."

After the two of them transferred Joni to her wheelchair and Judy left for the restroom, Joni said, "What's the matter?" Ken didn't reply, busying himself instead with the adjustment on her foot pedals.

"What's wrong?" she repeated.

He still didn't answer. Mr. Strong-and-Silent evidently wasn't going to talk to her. *That* would never do.

They were both relieved when Judy said good-bye outside and left for her own car. When they got to Joni's van, Ken turned his back to her and started to fiddle with the ramp.

"Wait!" Joni said. "I'm not going any further until you tell me what's wrong."

He turned to look at her, straightening his spine and folding his arms across his chest. (If he only knew how much he looked like "Mr. Clean" when he did that.) "OK," he said, "you were *talking* during the movie, and you didn't stop even after I said something."

"I'm not one of the kids in your classroom, Ken."

"You were disturbing people."

"Are you kidding? We were *whispering*. Besides, the place was practically empty."

"Look, I had just gotten up to tell those teenagers down in front to be quiet. And then you and Judy started doing the same thing!"

"We were NOT. We were whispering — not throwing popcorn and making a racket!"

"Don't yell at me!"

"You call *this* yelling? You haven't heard anything yet!"

"Well, I don't yell."

"Well, I *do*! Our whole family yells."

"I knew it."

"You knew what?"

"We get engaged, and then we become different people."

She tried to control her voice. "Ken, this is who I *am*. I'm not being different."

He stopped his pacing for a moment to turn to look at her. "Haven't you heard of those verses about being angry and sinning not? About letting no unwholesome words come out of your mouth?"

She was incredulous. Something absurdly minor had somehow mushroomed into something incredibly major. And he was suddenly pushing his expectations on her. This was making her very angry.

"Don't go throwing verses at me," she snapped. Powering up closer to him, she had a sudden urge to run over his feet! Look at him standing there like a statue again, with his arms folded. She had just opened her mouth to really give it to him when ...

"Excuse me." A young couple stepping through the twilight approached their van. "Aren't you the lady who draws with her mouth? Joanie? We heard you speak at my mother's church once."

She swallowed the verbal harpoon she had been about to hurl at Ken and pasted on a smile. It felt as cheap and phony as a piece of Monopoly money.

"Yes," she said, "I'm Joni. And this is Ken Tada, my fiancé."

They looked pleased and happy.

Ken extended his hand, somehow managing a weak smile, trying to mumble something appropriate. As he began answering questions about the upcoming wedding, Joni wondered if he was still all that excited about it.

They watched as the couple headed for the movie theater, holding hands and talking excitedly. "So, *Joanie* ..." he began, "what *did* you talk about at his mother's church?"

"Oh ... well," she said, avoiding his eyes. "I probably talked about my paralysis, and how it was helping me become more Christlike. You know ... being loving ... self-controlled ... patient ..."

He took a step toward her, his face relaxed into the Ken Tada smile that always made her heart beat faster.

"And," she said, raising her face to him with an answering smile, blinking back sudden tears, "and I still want to get married … if you do."

"I do," he said, wiping a tear from her face with a clean, folded handkerchief. "And that's good practice. *I do*."

SEPTEMBER 1987

Borrowing Ken's hands, she had just finished packing her bags for yet another ministry trip. Ken had already packed rods and reels and fishing gear for a trip of his own. They would be apart for several days, and they knew they'd miss each other.

Wheeling through the living room that afternoon, she stopped in her tracks as she noticed a beautiful red rose in a bud vase on the table. That Ken! What a thoughtful thing to think of. It warmed her heart.

Moving into the bedroom to gather her things, she spotted *another* red rose in a bud vase on her dressing table. *What in the world was he up to?* Quickly she glanced in the bathroom, and yes, there was yet another perfect red rose in another bud vase adorning the counter of her vanity.

With the third rose, her feelings of pleasure drained away. It wasn't that she didn't appreciate his gifts, but really, they were leaving in a few hours. Nobody but their miniature schnauzer, Scruffy, would be in the house to enjoy the roses — the *expensive* roses. Could they really afford to throw their money around like that?

Ken's big hug, however, melted away her protests, and she decided not to make an issue of the spending.

As she settled into her seat on the airplane, she thought about those roses, which of course was what Ken had hoped would happen all along.

Back when they were dating, he had flooded her with gifts. She had received more candles, stuffed animals, sweetheart cards, and vases of fresh yellow roses than she cared to remember. She had pleaded with him to lighten up, only to receive pink roses instead of yellow ones the next day. This was a man who wanted to show his love, even if it meant excess and sheer extravagance.

Extravagance. Wasn't that a mark of authentic love?

Her plane lifted into the skies above Southern California. She peered out the window, catching a glimpse of the Pacific, where Ken would soon be fishing.

Love was extravagant in the price it was willing to pay, the time it was willing to give, the hardships it was willing to endure, and the strength it was willing to spend.

That was certainly a picture of Ken.

That was certainly a picture of Jesus.

SUMMER 1988

They pitched their tent underneath a stand of tall pine trees near a stream, swiftly flowing with melted snow from the High Sierras.

Ken had been out with his fishing pole already and had caught and cleaned a couple of rainbow trout for breakfast. From the tent, she could smell them sizzling in the cast-iron frying pan over the campfire, mingling with the fragrances of pine trees and fresh coffee percolating in their old, fire-blackened percolator.

Even in midsummer, their high altitude camping spot was crisp and cold. Ken's eyes danced with pleasure as he came into the tent to get her up and dressed.

For Joni, camping meant a flannel shirt, dusty jeans, no makeup, and a scarf over her dirty hair. And it was glorious! Not all of her girlfriends appreciated camping the way she did. But her girlfriends hadn't been raised by a daddy who was an outdoors-man and was determined that his three daughters appreciate it as much as if they had been three sons.

They didn't do much. Ken would fish, and Joni would sit in the sun and read a good book. They might explore a trail or two or even rent a boat and row out into a mountain lake.

Now *that* was a glorious morning. The scenery was enough to pull the air right out of your lungs. The very essence of tranquillity! Drifting along in the sunshine, the water lap-lapping against the sides of the boat, the whir of Ken's fishing reel as he made a long cast, and the mountains soaring all around them like high sentinels.

She and Ken watched an eagle leave its nest in one of the rocky crags and sweep over the lake in search of breakfast. They had been reading in Job that morning, and she was reminded of the Lord's words to the old patriarch: "Does the hawk take flight by your wisdom and spread its wings toward the south? Does the eagle soar at your command and build its nest on high?" (Job 39:26 – 27).

It must have made Job feel very small to hear the Lord speak of so many great and mighty things that He accomplished every day in the wild places of the world. Small, but lost in God's greatness.

She felt small too, out in the middle of the wide, blue lake, in the great wilderness silence, ringed by towering old-growth pines and snow-capped mountains beyond that.

Small, but filled with wonder at God's greatness in the majesty of His creation.

Ken cast his line again, looked over at her, and smiled. And how kind of God to give her someone to share it all with.

FEBRUARY 1989

It was Sunday morning, and they'd had another argument.

What was it about Sundays and getting ready to go to church and worship the Lord that sparked so many disagreements? Maybe it was just the rush. Getting up, bolting down breakfast, gathering notebooks and Bibles, warming up the van, and all the thousand and one extra things they had to do for Joni because of her quadriplegia.

"You could've asked Judy to help you with your vest and scarf before she left." Ken mechanically stuffed Joni's arms through armholes and jerked hard to button the vest. "We're late as it is," he said in a low, tense voice. The brusqueness with which he treated her made her bristle.

"We're late because you didn't start taking a shower until twenty minutes ago," she said in a tone to match his.

"Oh, so it's *my* fault."

She was silent for a moment and then turned the dagger. "You said it, not me."

All the way down the freeway toward church, a frosty silence hung between them. Ken took the exit to Las Virgenes Road a little too fast and braked a little too hard at the stoplight. It jostled her, but she stubbornly refused to say anything. It might have been a bright California winter day outside, but inside the van it felt dark and gloomy.

Both of them dreaded being the first to speak up and break the impasse. But what they dreaded even more was sitting together in God's house, singing hymns and reading Scripture when their hearts felt locked up from irritation and hurt.

They pulled into the parking lot with a few minutes to spare before the start of the service. But both of them felt like they would have preferred to simply turn the van around and go home. Ken turned off the motor, and they sat in silence, listening to the pops and cracks of the stilled engine.

Ken looked at her in the rearview mirror. "Can we pray?"

"I don't really feel like it."

"Neither do I, but ... maybe that's the time when we need it most."

He waited for a long moment, and then he opened his Bible to Romans 8 and read about how the Holy Spirit would help them in their weakness when they didn't feel like praying or even know what to say. Then he closed the Bible, and they closed their eyes ... and waited. The windows in the van were up, yet they could still hear the strains of a hymn from inside the church. Joni began to hum along. And within a moment or two, scarves and vests and being late didn't seem all that important.

And the Holy Spirit kept His promise.

JUNE 1990

"There's a full moon tonight," Ken said as they were cleaning up the dishes from supper. "Want to go for a walk?"

"Oh, boy, let's do it!"

"But remember, it's June. We have to wait for a while until it gets dark."

A full moon on a June night in Southern California was definitely worth waiting for.

Joni, of course, could get poetic about it. In one of her books she wrote about "the silvery sheen of a bright moonlit night when the shadows are long and common shapes and figures take on an almost magical quality."

Ken, never quite so poetic, just enjoyed setting aside his lesson plans and getting out in the cooler night air. They walked together on the sidewalk, Joni in her power chair and Ken resting a hand on her shoulder, one of the few places where she could feel that husbandly touch.

A few others were out too, walking dogs or watering flowerbeds, but most of the Californians had gone inside for the night.

"Did I ever tell you how we'd go out on full-moon nights back on the farm?" Joni said.

"I think so. But tell me again."

"I was going to anyway."

"I thought so."

"We would saddle up horses and go for a moonlit ride. Daddy and his four girls — can you imagine?"

"Just barely."

"We'd go riding down the gravel road, all silver in the moonlight. I can still hear the clop-clop of the horses' hooves. We'd laugh and sing funny, romantic songs about the moon. 'Oh, Mr. Moon, moon, bright and silvery moon, won't you please shine down on me?'" she sang in rhythm with Ken's walk.

"It was a bit different from the way I grew up. There weren't too many moonlit horseback rides in Burbank."

"I know. But anyway, here we are, together under a full moon in Calabasas. It's still pretty magical."

"Yes," he said, smiling over at her, "it sure is."

OCTOBER 2000

She had been getting ready for a speaking engagement at a prestigious conference, and it was definitely "a big deal." It was one of those exclusive, by-invitation-only affairs populated by corporate executives, trustees from various foundations and colleges, and presidents of major universities.

With the help of several of her team members, she had worked to get her message "just right." Judy had helped her find a new outfit to wear, and someone else had volunteered to clean and polish her wheelchair.

OK, so these were just people who, in the big scheme of things, were no more "important" than other people. But even so ... why not try to be at her very, very best?

Just three days before she was due to fly out to the conference, something happened that had never happened before. She had been wheeling along outside when she began to feel a thump-thump-thump jostling of her chair. *What in the world ... ?*

Glancing over her shoulder she saw with incredulous eyes that the tire of her wheelchair had split apart. All the foam inside was spilling out into a big, ugly growth on the side of her tire. It looked ... grotesque ... horrible. She knew that if she didn't do something soon, she would soon be riding on the rims of her wheels. Images came to her mind of wild police car chases in Los Angeles with fleeing vehicles careening down surface streets on shot-out tires, the rims digging into the asphalt and sending up showers of sparks.

Ken would know what to do.

She called him, and he gravely examined the problem, hurried into the garage, and came back with ... a roll of duct tape.

His beloved, jumbo, silver-hued, do-everything, fix-anything duct tape.

She looked at him in disbelief. "Duct tape?" she said. "You're going to fix my tire with *duct tape*?"

Ken explained that until he could order a new tire, it was their only option. With that, he began to wrap her bulging, misshapen tire — and that lovely, shining rim — with layer after layer of duct tape.

Was that a little smile on his face he was trying to hide? Was he actually enjoying himself? He'd better not be!

Round and round he wound the tape until the bulge was completely contained.

"OK," he said, "try wheeling on it."

Joni powered her chair slowly forward. It was still going thump-thump-thump, but at least the rim was safe. It had worked, after a fashion, *and it was incredibly tacky.*

"Best I can do for now," Ken had said, still basking in the glow of his accomplishment.

"Oh, no," Joni groaned. "I can't believe I've got to roll thump-thump-thump in front of the audience — *that* audience — looking like I've just been in a demolition derby."

Ken smiled at that image in spite of himself, and Joni couldn't help but smile back (just a little). It was another example of God not allowing her to become too self-focused or overly impressed with herself.

He had always had a way of keeping her humble.

And to be fair, the duct tape *had* worked.

SEPTEMBER 2004

It was to be Joni and Ken's longest and most rigorous trip ever. First, it was a two-day flight to India, with a stopover in London. Then, after five days spent ministering in Bangalore, they flew to Bangkok, Thailand, for a conference on world evangelization. From there, it was a twenty-one-hour flight from Bangkok to Dubai, and finally on to Addis Ababa, Ethiopia.

The capital city was modern and bustling, but just a mile beyond the city border lay clusters of thatched huts and crumbling concrete houses. Ancient Coptic churches were speckled throughout tightly clustered neighborhoods, while newly built mosques cast long shadows over homes and shops. The mosques all seemed empty. That's when their Christian host explained. "The imams say, 'Your children may play in the shadow of these minarets now, but one day, *their* children will be ours.'" Ethiopia was the only "Christian" nation in Sahara Africa, and it was obvious that Muslims were making a concerted effort to claim it as theirs.

The week was busy with meetings with pastors, appointments with disability and government leaders, a visit to a leprosy clinic, and a press conference, but Joni and Ken were especially looking forward to speaking at a large public meeting in the downtown soccer hall — a large rectangular structure made entirely of steel and tin. Although the clouds looked dark and threatening on the morning of the event, it certainly didn't dissuade people from coming. By the time Ken and Joni arrived, their van had to putter its way down a pockmarked dirt road through thick crowds to reach the entrance.

"These people — all of them — are so beautiful," Joni remarked, looking out the window. When Ken lifted her out of the van and into her wheelchair, large groups simply stood and watched. Some women covered their faces with their veils — that's when they remembered that their host said there would be many Muslims in the audience that day.

It meant that, once she was on the platform, Joni wanted to be very succinct in not only explaining the gospel of Christ but also in helping these people understand Jesus' compassion for people with disabilities. She recalled how earlier, the crowds — wanting to watch Ken help her — had shoved aside women in wheelchairs and men on crutches. "No, please, let them come forward!" she cried, but she wasn't sure they understood.

When she wheeled into position on the platform and looked up, it took her breath away. In front of her stretched a sea of thousands of faces filling the aisles all the way to the back of the hall.

She took a deep breath and began, telling her story as simply as she could, speaking about her "black heart," her need of a Savior, and how Jesus Christ won the right to be her substitute on the cross. She then described Jesus' love for the weak and needy, especially for those with disabilities.

"Jesus told us to go out and find these people, and to bring them in. Everyone wants to be treated with dignity and respect, especially when you have a disability," she said, gesturing to her own wheelchair.

As she was about to wind up her message, the clouds above the soccer hall burst open and rain poured down on the tin roof. *Thank you, Lord, for letting me finish*, she thought with great relief.

It wasn't easy getting back to their van, but Ken and Joni were in no rush. They paused often to give hugs and thank the people. The rain made the late afternoon darker than usual, and once they reached the door, it looked like it would be a mad dash to reach the van without getting wet. Their hosts, however, were ready with umbrellas. They shook the rain off their coats, started the engine, flipped on the windshield wipers, and began to slowly drive back to the main highway, swerving this way and that to avoid potholes and groups of people walking in the downpour.

Suddenly, their headlights caught the back of a young woman inching along, drenched to the bone and valiantly maneuvering her wheelchair through the mud. Scores of people passed her, holding newspapers over their heads and simply walking around her. No one stopped to offer help or push her wheelchair. Joni leaned forward in her chair to get a good look. "I can't believe this — all this, after I just finished talking about God's compassion for us ... And how we must show that same compassion to others!"

Watching this disabled woman struggle was too much to bear.

"Stop!" Ken called out. "Stop here!" Ken tore off his sport coat, rolled up the sleeves of his clean, starched shirt, and hopped out of the van. "Here, take an umbrella!" someone in the back called, but Ken waved them off. Hopping over rain puddles in his good shoes, he found the handles of the woman's wheelchair and threw his weight against it. All the way to the main road, in the pouring rain, he carefully steered the woman around people, rocks, and ruts.

Joni swelled with admiration for her husband! And she half hoped that someone would come alongside to help, lend a hand, and put into practice the point of her message. But it didn't happen. By the time they reached the main road, everyone was scattering in different directions. Ken, who left the woman by the bus stop, had never met a more grateful person! She turned her chair in the direction of the van, calling out, "Thank you! Thank you!" and waving with all her might. Which was especially poignant, explained their host, because it was likely that two or three buses would turn her down before she caught one that would allow her to board.

Ken hopped in the van and brushed off his hair. "I think she still has far to go."

No doubt, thought Joni. *But at least for once in her life a good man cared enough to help her along the way.*

DECEMBER 2010

Chemotherapy was finally over. The fiercest part of the battle against cancer was behind them. At last, they could relax a little and reminisce, finding humor in the nastiest of experiences.

One of the things Dr. Ashouri had warned them about was the way chemo drugs could weaken bones. Joni's were already thin and fragile. So in late December, he scheduled her for a regular scan to measure the density of her bones.

How tough could that be?

As they headed to the hospital, they were wondering, *Can a bone scan be all that complicated?* For most patients it meant slipping on a surgical gown, hopping on the table, and taking a ten-minute nap while the scanner did its thing. That's the way it was for most people, but most people aren't quadriplegics.

First, the scanner was in the *tiniest* of rooms into which Ken had to manhandle her wheelchair. It was the size of a closet, made even smaller by the two male aides who had to squeeze in to help lift Joni. Heaving his wife onto the table was no easy feat, and then he nearly wrenched his back uncorseting her and pulling off her slacks.

"Ken, catch my arm, please. It's falling off the table."

"Got it!" He then turned his attention to her leg bag and began taking it off.

"There it goes again!"

"Come on, arms," he said, "work with me here!" He retrieved it again and then had an idea. He tucked her elbows tightly against her hips with a draw sheet. After that, he lined up her body with the machine and called in the technician. The ten-minute scan was a breeze — it was getting dressed and back into the wheelchair that took three times as long.

But that's life; that's "normal" for a quadriplegic.

This bone scan? It was a cinch compared to what they had been through. It was funny how suffering became so relative. What used to be "unbearable" became endurable compared to the worst of times. And all of it was geared by God to remind them of their total dependence on Him.

The struggle with the bone scan was simply a reminder of their urgent, drastic dependence on God. Jesus had referred to it in the gospel of John: "I am the vine; you are the branches. Whoever abides in me and I in him, he it is that bears much fruit, for apart from me you can do nothing" (John 15:5 ESV).

Vines and branches don't separate. It's impossible for them to do so. In the same way, there could be no "disconnect" when it came to abiding in Christ.

Joni had thought about that the week before the scan. Too many times she had found herself thinking, *How long do I have to be plugged into God through a quiet time or prayer or reading a book to get the charge I need to then go out and do my thing?* But Jesus had never said, "I am the power cord; you are the iPhone."

He said, "I am the vine; you are the branches." If she wanted that life — and she did — there couldn't be any disconnect. Abiding was what desperate people did who realized they had no life, no power, no resource within themselves.

After the bone scan, they wheeled out into the parking lot and ... laughed. Not that it had been easy. Far from it. But relative to everything else, it was a walk in the park. Hard? Yes. Frustrating? You bet. Pushing them up against the grace of God? Always! But could they — *would* they — deal with it again?

No doubt!

"You do understand," she said to Ken, "that we'll have to do more of these in the future, right?"

"Sure," he replied, cranking the van's ignition. "But we'll know how to tackle it better next time."

"What do you have in mind?"

Ken kept a straight face. "It's simple. We order an industrial crane with a hoist capacity of ... oh, say, about *a hundred tons.*"

Joni laughed. "OK, Mr. Ken Takeshi Tada," she said from the back of the van, "you're in *big* trouble now."

"Am I? Well, guess what? I've been there before," he said, glancing in the rearview mirror with a smile. "And I lived to tell the story!"

A PERSONAL NOTE FROM JONI AND KEN

Two are better than one,
    because they have a good return for their labor:
If either of them falls down,
    one can help the other up.
But pity anyone who falls
    and has no one to help them up.
Also, if two lie down together, they will keep warm.
    But how can one keep warm alone?
Though one may be overpowered,
    two can defend themselves.
A cord of three strands is not quickly broken.

ECCLESIASTES 4:9 – 12

It's funny, but I have a hard time these days just writing "Joni."

I always want to write "Joni and Ken."

No, not as though it were stamped on a wedding napkin or written on a house mortgage document. It's more visceral than that. Thirty years have passed since Ken and I began our journey together, and God has used every trial — every hurt and heartache — to entwine us far more intimately than we ever dreamed on the day we married.

And the more devastating the trials, the more He has wrapped us both around Himself. God has used depression and chronic pain and cancer — far more than even quadriplegia — to bind us tighter than ever. To each other. To Him.

That's the "cord of three strands" the Bible speaks about. Husband, wife, and the Lord Himself. If the man and woman twine their lives around each other in marriage, that is good, and they'll be stronger for it. But if both of them twine themselves around the living God, that's best of all. It's a union that will hold through anything that life — or even hell — might throw at them.

It's a beautiful picture, but we know it isn't true for everyone. It's especially difficult for couples dealing with a serious disability. So many of these marriages just don't survive the test. The fact is, we live in a society that doesn't know what to do with suffering. We do everything we can think of to escape it: we medicate it, mask it, surgically remove it, entertain or drug it, institutionalize it, divorce it, or even euthanize it — anything but live with it. Suffering, however, isn't about to go away. And marriage only magnifies it.

It's why we hope this book has inspired you. A *visceral* inspiration. Because nowhere else — and with no one else — will you have quite the chance to experience union with Christ than through a hard-fought-for, hard-won union with your spouse. And although Ken and I don't pretend to be experts, we've learned enough to feel confident about passing on a couple of encouragements ...

If I were sitting next to you this very moment ... wherever you are ... I know what I would say to you. I would say, "Oh, please *pray* for your partner." Hands down, it beats any how-to marriage manual or nationally renowned couples' conference. Pray that your husband or your wife will eventually join you in prayer. I don't mean a stiff formality carried out on Sunday or before bed or at meals. I mean praying anywhere at any time about anything. Out loud. With hearts engaged. And doing it together. When husbands and wives join hands and talk to God, tight and uncomfortable trials suddenly become a "signal": *Aha!*

We should pray about this! It's trials that really press you into the breast of your Savior.

The cord of three strands.

Next, realize that your enemy is *not* your spouse or even the disability or the bankruptcy or the disagreement or whatever it is that is troubling you.

The enemy is Satan himself.

He hates marriage, and he has hated it since the very first such union in a fragrant, misty garden called Eden. This fierce adversary will do everything in his power to suffocate married love. So be alert! Keep casting yourself on Jesus Christ, steadily relying on Him, even when you don't feel like it.

And when things feel overwhelming? That is the time to *make* yourself ask for help. God never intended for marriage partners to be isolated from other believers. Besides, asking for help keeps you humble, and we all know that humility keeps the Devil at bay.

Oh, how I wish I could park my wheelchair near you and whisper even more uplifting and hopeful words into your heart. How I wish Ken could flip open his journal and show you what his buddies wrote to urge him on. But the best word of all to leave you with? The Word of Life — Jesus Christ. His words, and His alone, will bring healing to your weary heart, strength into your tiring routines, and peace for your tangled thoughts. His Word will be that sharp-edged sword that will convict you when pride puffs you up. Or be that soft blanket that comforts you when pain leaves you feeling wounded.

A picture is always worth more than the words sitting on a printed page. And we've got one for you.

A complete and authoritative lexicon on marriage is summed up in a two-minute video on YouTube.[14] Nothing fancy or flowery. Just an elderly man with gray hair and glasses, dressed in a plaid cotton shirt, shooting pool and the breeze as his wife, Jean, sits looking on, slumped in her recliner wheelchair. The scene is in their assisted living center.

Dr. Mounce, former president of Whitworth College, speaks

tenderly of his wife who deals with severe dementia. "Marriage has a way of getting better," he says. "In a sense, the best life is a life that's invested in someone else. It's not a life invested in yourself ... love is placing the welfare of another in front of your own."

The camera captures him tenderly feeding Jean. "When we first moved here, we moved into an apartment, and at that time she was failing a bit. As things got worse and I could no longer do her care, she moved into the health center. That was almost two years ago, but I'm with her most of the time. So we read and go out, like yesterday, for a ride in the car."

Dr. Mounce plays a baby grand piano with Jean, again, sitting and looking on.

But the next scene is what grips me most. Robert is reading the Bible by Jean's bedside. *Entertainment Tonight* drones in another room, and a glow from the fluorescent light above the bed softens the scene. He continues. "Jean sometimes says, 'I want to go home.' And I have to tell her that home is where we are together. Home is movable. So when we're in her room, we're home. When we're in my apartment, that's home. Home is together."

Ken and I are nowhere near the age of Robert and Jean Mounce. Nor have we been married as long. But my heart leaps in recognition when he says, "Home is movable ... Home is together." It's the goal of any marriage, and perhaps the singular indicator of a successful one. And although Ken and I probably don't meet all the family-counseling criteria for "a happy marriage," this I know for sure ...

Home is with him.

Home is with Ken Tada.

If you asked Ken, he'd say the same. *Home is wherever we are together.*

It's why this book was written. For many people, maybe *most* people, I think all of our lives are spent looking for and wanting to go home. But what if it were as close as the hand of your spouse? *That* would make for a contented and complete marriage.

What you hold in your hands is a record of the arduous journey it took for Ken and me to smile at each other and say with all our hearts, "There's no place like home." And it's our prayer that this modest little book will provide a few signposts to point you in the same direction.

Hang in there, friend. Life will not always be this hard, or marriage so difficult. There is coming a Day when something so grand and glorious will appear that it will supersede even marriage. Heaven is on the horizon for us all, and what we do down here on earth — every little drastic obedience — all of it will one day have a direct bearing on our capacity for joy and for worship and service in heaven. If you stick close to Jesus and honor Him through the toughest of times, you have a better chance of casting more crowns at His feet. And one day, when you touch His nail-scarred hands to say *thank You*, you'll have every confidence He'll know you mean it. He will recognize you as the one who persevered, who took up your cross daily to redeem the hard places in your marriage, just as He once took up His cross to redeem you.

The Day is soon coming when you will see the stunningly glorified version of your spouse. No, you won't be joined in marriage in heaven, but God will have used your earthly life together to prepare you to be friends, yes, to be sisters and brothers — special and unique — for all of eternity. So get a jump start on eternity with that friend now.

Take a deep breath, and let *it* — whatever that irksome *it* is in your marriage — let it go. Make a covenant. Renew the vows. Get out the candles and china. Order the roses. Dim the lights. Walk under the stars. Quit resisting and start affirming. After all, loving that one to whom you said yes, well … it's just another way, maybe the *best* way, of loving and serving God.

ACKNOWLEDGMENTS

Larry Libby and I have written more than a few books together, but this one is different. As you've already discovered, it's written from a third-person perspective. An outsider looking in. A muse on our shoulders, capturing moments and insights we might miss if I were holding the pen, which would be a feat in itself, given my quadriplegia. In preparation for this book, Ken and I threw everything at Larry we possibly could — articles, messages, blogs, interviews, e-mails, radio transcripts, out-of-print books of mine, you name it.

After his wife, Carol, sifted through and organized everything, Larry, with skill and finesse, was able to shape the material into an artful exposé of "life with Joni and Ken." Thank you, Larry, for the wonderfully natural way you write — I've learned everything I know about cadence and clarity, style and substance, from you. And a special thanks to Carol, your biggest cheerleader.

Ken and I are just as indebted to our good friends at Zondervan. This team of experts bent over backward to make this book a unique offering on the bookshelf. It was John Sloan, my longtime editor, who convinced Larry and me that a third-person perspective would make *Joni and Ken: An Untold Love Story* read more easily. It didn't take long to convince us. And a special thanks to Scott, Alicia, Bob, and so many more — ever since they published the *Joni* book in 1976, Zondervan has felt like family.

We especially thank the fine team at Wolgemuth & Associates, who championed the idea of *Joni and Ken: An Untold Love*

Story long before a word was written. Robert and Bobbie Wolgemuth, Andrew and Erik Wolgemuth, Susan Kreider, and we can't forget Austin Wilson — this amazing, well-seasoned company has gone to bat for Ken and me time and again. They worry about book stuff … we just write.

We are exceedingly grateful to the staff of Joni and Friends, led by our president and COO Mr. Doug Mazza. Our headquarters at the Joni and Friends International Disability Center is the most peaceful, pleasant place in the world you'd ever want to work. And, I might add, write. I bless my coworkers who kept me in their prayers. I thank my executive assistant Judy Butler, who kept my schedule clear, and longtime secretary Francie Lorey, for happily serving as my "hands" at the keyboard. (Francie, *Dragon Naturally Speaking* will never, ever replace you!)

If Ken were sitting next to me right now as I compose this paragraph, he'd want to pay honor to two exceptional friends — Pete Lubisich and Jan Janura. During my bout with cancer, these gentlemen were *there*, ministering to and mentoring him with daily phone calls, notes, and prayers. Ken is a richer man for their friendship. Every guy should have companions like Pete and Jan.

Most of all, we thank the many couples who are hanging in there, despite dealing with tough disabilities. These are the men and women who inspire us greatly. They attend our Joni and Friends' Family Retreats, serve on our staff, and lead by example. And here are just a few of our favorite "quad couples": Jess and Sib Charles, Jerry and Joan Borton (OK, Jerry, so you're not quite a quad), Curtis and Carol Hoke, Tom and Marla Horton, Mike and Renee Bondi, Doug and Lynn Wheeler, Chuck and Alice Heidel, Don and Elaine Scholes. And so many more. These couples know what adversity tastes like. They experience the weariness of day-after-day routines. Yet they persevere and hold fast to Jesus. We are honored to be in the fellowship of sharing in Christ's sufferings alongside them.

Finally, I thank my wonderful life partner, Ken Tada. He diligently prayed for Larry Libby and for me, always encouraging, always there with "a pat on the back." I guess he is the real inspiration behind *Joni and Ken: An Untold Love Story.* Because the "untold" part of this book is actually all about Ken.

In many ways, it is *his* story.

Thank you, dear Ken.

RESOURCES FOR YOU

For a complete list of other books written by Joni Eareckson Tada, or for more information about her greeting cards, which she paints by mouth, visit the website of the Joni and Friends International Disability Center at www.joniandfriends.org.

Or you can write Joni and Ken at:

Joni and Friends International Disability Center
PO Box 3333
Agoura Hills, CA 91376, USA
818-707-5664

The mission of Joni and Friends is to communicate the gospel and equip Christ-honoring churches worldwide to evangelize and disciple people affected by disability. Premiere programs include Wheels for the World, Family Retreats, the Joni and Friends television series, and a radio outreach aired on more than one thousand outlets across America.

The Christian Institute on Disability is the educational and training arm of Joni and Friends, partnering with Christian universities and seminaries around the world to develop courses of study in disability ministry. Through a network of volunteers and Area Ministry teams, Joni and Friends works on a local level to accelerate Christian ministry into the disability community around the world.

If you have a disability in your family, we urge you to prayerfully consider attending a Joni and Friends Family Retreat near you. The ministry holds over twenty Family Retreats across the

United States every summer, with additional Family Retreats in developing nations.

If you have benefited from Joni and Ken's story, let them know by writing Joni and Friends today. We would love to hear your story and learn how we can pray for you. You'll also be encouraged by reading other books written by Joni Eareckson Tada. Joni and Friends is here to serve you!

NOTES

1. "Don't Get Around Much Anymore," lyrics by Bob Russell (1942).

2. "For the lonely: 150 songs for sobbing on Valentine's Day," Pop & Hiss: The L.A. Times Music Blog, February 13, 2009, http://latimesblogs.latimes.com/music_blog/valentines_day/ (accessed August 6, 2012).

3. "Volare," lyrics by Franco Migliacci and Domenico Modugno (1958).

4. "Sweet Hour of Prayer," lyrics by William W. Walford (1845).

5. "A Mighty Fortress Is Our God," lyrics by Martin Luther (1529).

6. "Blessed Assurance, Jesus Is Mine!" lyrics by Fanny J. Crosby (1873).

7. Second Corinthians 10:5.

8. Rick Warren, *The Purpose Driven Life* (Grand Rapids: Zondervan, 2002), 17.

9. Ray Bradbury, *The October Country* (New York: HarperCollins, 1999), 1.

10. First Corinthians 2:2.

11. "Higher Ground," lyrics by Johnson Oatman Jr. (1898).

12. Quoted in Steve Israel, ed., *Charge! History's Greatest Military Speeches* (Annapolis, Md.: Naval Institute Press, 2007), 205.

13. "All the Way My Savior Leads Me," lyrics by Fanny J. Crosby (1875).

14. "Thoughts on Love and Care," YouTube, www.youtube.com/watch?v=Ro2bork7XIE (accessed August 22, 2012).

Joni

An Unforgettable Story

Joni Eareckson Tada

The award-winning story of a young woman who triumphed over devastating odds to touch countless lives the world over with the healing message of Christ. With all-new 16-page full-color photo insert, including drawings by Joni.

In a split second on a hot July afternoon, a diving accident transformed the life of Joni Eareckson Tada forever. She went from being an active young woman to facing every day in a wheelchair. In this unforgettable autobiography, Joni reveals each step of her struggle to accept her disability and discover the meaning of her life. The hard-earned truths she discovers and the special ways God reveals his love are testimonies to faith's triumph over hardship and suffering. This edition of Joni's heartwarming story—which has more than 3,000,000 copies in print in over forty languages—will introduce a new generation of readers to the amazing greatness of God's power and mercy at work in those who fully give their hearts and lives to him. Joni's afterword describes the events that have occurred in her life since the book's original publication in 1976, including her marriage to Ken Tada and the expansion of her worldwide ministry to families affected by disability. *Joni* is also available in an unabridged audio version read by the author.

Available in stores and online!

Diamonds in the Dust
366 Sparkling Devotions
Joni Eareckson Tada

With more than 200,000 copies sold, *Diamonds in the Dust* has become a devotional favorite. Joni shows us precious jewels of biblical truth that lie scattered amid the gravel of life's dusty road.

More Precious Than Silver
366 Daily Devotional Readings
Joni Eareckson Tada

More Precious Than Silver reveals surpassing wealth in the subtle things we overlook as we chase life's golden glitter. This year's worth of wise, insightful devotions will show you why nothing can compare to the riches of a heart that has known the silver touch of God's Word. Includes photos and drawings by Joni.

Pearls of Great Price
366 Daily Devotional Readings
Joni Eareckson Tada

In the tradition of *Diamonds in the Dust* and *More Precious Than Silver* comes this book, *Pearls of Great Price*. Written by a remarkable woman who has known firsthand God's faithfulness in the midst of indescribable difficulties, these 366 inspiring new devotions, each filled with Joni's signature storytelling, will touch your soul like a genuine pearl—rare, beautiful, and precious.

When God Weeps

Why Our Sufferings Matter to the Almighty

Joni Eareckson Tada
and Steven Estes

If God is loving, why is there suffering?

What's the difference between permitting something and ordaining it?

When bad things happen, who's behind them — God or the devil?

When suffering touches our lives, questions like these suddenly demand an answer. From our perspective, suffering doesn't make sense, especially when we believe in a loving and just God.

After more than forty years in a wheelchair, Joni Eareckson Tada's intimate experience with suffering gives her a special understanding of God's intentions for us in our pain. In *When God Weeps*, Joni and lifelong friend Steven Estes probe beyond glib answers that fail us in our time of deepest need. Instead, with firmness and compassion, they reveal a God big enough to understand our suffering, wise enough to allow it — and powerful enough to use it for a greater good than we can ever imagine

Heaven

Your Real Home

Joni Eareckson Tada

Step back a moment, focus your eyes of faith, and then come with Joni into a world you've heard about from your youth but have never seen: heaven. You just might discover that heaven is closer — and more real — than you've ever thought.

In this joyful bestseller, Joni Eareckson Tada paints a shining portrait of our heart's true home. She talks about what heaven will be like, what we'll do, and whom we'll see. Joni shows how heaven will be the satisfaction of all that our hearts cry for, something more real than anything this side of eternity.

And Joni tells how we can prepare now for the reality of heaven.

With hope for today and vision for those who struggle in life, *Heaven* invites us to a refreshing and faith-filled picture of our glorious destination. Once you've caught a glimpse of heaven, you'll see earth in a whole new light.

Available in stores and online!

Share Your Thoughts

With the Author: Your comments will be forwarded to the author when you send them to *zauthor@zondervan.com*.

With Zondervan: Submit your review of this book by writing to *zreview@zondervan.com*.

Free Online Resources at
www.zondervan.com

Zondervan AuthorTracker: Be notified whenever your favorite authors publish new books, go on tour, or post an update about what's happening in their lives at www.zondervan.com/authortracker.

Daily Bible Verses and Devotions: Enrich your life with daily Bible verses or devotions that help you start every morning focused on God. Visit www.zondervan.com/newsletters.

Free Email Publications: Sign up for newsletters on Christian living, academic resources, church ministry, fiction, children's resources, and more. Visit www.zondervan.com/newsletters.

Zondervan Bible Search: Find and compare Bible passages in a variety of translations at www.zondervanbiblesearch.com.

Other Benefits: Register to receive online benefits like coupons and special offers, or to participate in research.

ZONDERVAN

ZONDERVAN.com/
AUTHORTRACKER
follow your favorite authors